OF THESE YE MAY FREELY EAT

A Vegetarian Cookbook

by

JoAnn Rachor

FAMILY HEALTH PUBLICATIONS
13062 Musgrove Hwy.
Sunfield, MI 48890

Printed by
MMI PRESS
HARRISVILLE, NH 03450

LAWS OF HEALTH – AN INESTIMABLE BLESSING

The wonderful mechanism of the human body does not receive half the care that is often given to a mere lifeless machine. Man was the crowning act of the creation of God, made in the image of God, and designed to be a counterpart of God. Man is very dear to God because he was formed in His own image. God is the owner of the whole man. Soul, body and spirit are His. He gave His only begotten Son for the body as well as the soul, and our entire life belongs to Him, to be consecrated to His service, that through the exercise of every faculty He has given, we may glorify Him. From the first dawn of reason, the human mind should become intelligent in regard to the physical structure. We may behold and admire the work of God in the natural world, but the human habitation is the most wonderful. The laws governing the physical nature are as truly divine in their origin and character as the law of the ten commandments. Man is fearfully and wonderfully made; for Jehovah has inscribed His law by His own mighty hand on every part of the human body. Those who understand something of the wisdom and beneficence of His laws, and perceive the evidences of God's love and the blessings that result from obedience, will come to regard their duties and obligations from an altogether different point of view. Instead of looking upon the observance of the laws of health as a matter of sacrifice and self-denial, they will regard it as it really is, AN INESTIMABLE BLESSING.

(thoughts from the writings
of Ellen G. White)

"Something better is the watchword of education, the law of all true living. Whatever Christ asks us to renounce He offers in its stead something better." Ellen G. White, Education, p. 296.

TABLE OF CONTENTS

JoAnn Rachor
Family Health Publications
13062 Musgrove. Hwy.
Sunfield, Mich. 48890

ABOUT THE AUTHOR...

Although JoAnn Rachor has a degree in home economics and nutrition, her real qualification comes from the numerous cooking seminars she has given, and years of creative kitchen chemistry. As a former associate manager at the natural healing center at Uchee Pines Institute in Alabama, JoAnn gained first-hand knowledge in creating attractive menus for people with health problems. At the time of printing, she and her husband are doing health education and Christian missionary work based in Ft. Payne, Alabama.

DEFINITIONS OF LESS COMMON TERMS
AND INGREDIENTS

AGAR FLAKES - A dried sea weed used for thickening.

BERRIES - This is the term applied to the whole grain
kernel which has had nothing but cleaning done
to it after harvesting.

BLEND - To use an electric blender to make food smooth
or fine. The key to a smooth product is having just
enough liquid, along with solid ingredients, to
allow blades to barely turn. If a large amount of
liquid is blended with a small amount of solids the
end product will be chunky. Approximately equal
amounts of solid and liquid will give a smooth
consistency. Blending may take a full minute.
Don't rush.

BRAN - Recipes call for raw bran not commercial box
cereal.

BREAD CRUMBS, GROUND - Place broken pieces of bread
in blender and blend until fine.

CAROB - Healthful chocolate substitute. Purchased as
a flour or powder. Low fat.

CASHEWS, RINSED - Caution on all nuts from foreign
countries. They should be rinsed under hot water
before using, may follow by sterilization in oven
300° for 15 minutes.

CHICKEN OR BEEF STYLE SEASONING - Mixture of herbs
that give a meat flavor with no meat added. Brands
available are McKay's and Loma Linda or you can
make your own. These recipes use McKay's or the
recipe for *Chicken Style Seasoning* found in this
book. Loma Linda seasoning is not as strong.

COCONUT - Unsweetened type is recommended.

COFFEE SUBSTITUTE - Made from roasted grains and
seasonings, without caffeine. In small amounts,
dry, they give richness to certain recipes,
usually carob. Is generally considered an optional
ingredient in these recipes. Brands include
Caffix, Pero and Postum.

DEXTRINIZE - See Index.

Italics indicate item in index

DRIED FRUIT - When recipe simply calls for *dried fruit* use the fruits available or ones you enjoy most.

HOT, COOKED CEREAL, (i.e., millet, rice, cornmeal) - Must be hot to congeal, chill several hours before serving.

LEMON JUICE - Used in place of vinegar.

NUTS OR SEEDS - Nuts and seeds are interchangeable in these recipes. Nuts most versatile are cashews and almonds. Peanuts, walnuts, pecans and brazil nuts are fine but have a slightly stronger flavor. Sesame and sunflower seeds are most economical and quite acceptable in the recipes. Nuts and seeds are more nutritious if raw or dry roasted. They supply tenderness and flavor, often in place of oil.

OIL & LECITHIN - Excellent non-stick solution for bread pans, cookie sheets, waffle iron, etc. Shake together 1 part oil to 1 part liquid lecithin. Store in jar.

OIL, OPT (optional) - Oil in refined state is seldom, if ever, needed by an individual for added nutrition.

ONION & GARLIC POWDER - Inexpensive through food coops, buy in bulk, many uses.

ORANGE PEEL - Save unsprayed orange peel, dry in oven at low temp, blend when dry.

SESAME SEEDS - Available two ways: Hulled is white and has more mild flavor than the unhulled (brown color). Both are fine for cooking.

SOAKED SOYBEANS (or other beans) - Raw beans covered with three times as much water and soaked 8 hours or more. Then generally blended with water to use as a leavening agent. Or to replace oil for tenderness.

SOY BASE - Gives added richness and flavor. Made from either soybeans or soy flour. See recipe.

SOY MILK POWDER - A commercially prepared powder made from soybeans. Mix with water for a drink. Or use in powdered form in recipes to add richness and sweetening. There are several brand names. *Soyagen* is used in the recipes in this book.

Italics indicate item in index

3

SOY SAUCE - A highly salted seasoning. Use sparingly. If using, purchase unfermented soy sauce. LaChoy, the standard brand, is unfermented. Read the label. If it says aged or fermented do not use, ex. Tamari. See index for homemade *Soy Sauce.*

SWEETENER - Nutritionally there is very little difference in honey, molasses, corn syrup, white or brown sugar. The key is strict moderation. Therefore in recipes where *sweetener* is called for use whatever is available from the items listed above.

TAHINI - Nut butter, like peanut butter, made from hulled sesame seeds.

TOFU - A mild tasting soft curd made from soybeans.

WHOLE GRAIN FLOUR - Some of these can be made nicely in a blender. These include rolled or flaked cereals (i.e., oats, barley, rice, rye, wheat, soy), cracked wheat, millet, rice. Grains which do not have the outer shell or hull removed, called berries (i.e., wheat, rye, barley), can not be done well in blender.

YEAST FLAKES - Not baking yeast for raising bread. Gives foods a cheesy flavor. If using powdered yeast, reduce amount called for in recipe by half.

YEAST PASTE - A concentraded vegetable paste seasoning made primarily from soy, salt and *yeast flakes.* Commercial brands available include Vegex, Sovex, and Savorex. Or make your own from the recipe in this cookbook.

ZWIEBACK - See index.

Some of these items can be purchased in a supermarket but many will only be available through a food coop, health food store or market that sells such items. Look into starting a food coop and buy these items in bulk to save money.

Italics indicate item in index

B R E A D S
(Quick)

These quick or unleavened breads are made without baking powder or baking soda. These items leave residues in the breads that injure the body, or they damage the grains during the cooking process, making them less nourishing.

OAT CRACKERS

1½ c. quick or rolled oats	1/2 t. salt
1 c. flour	1/3 c. oil
1/2 c. wheat germ or *raw bran*	2/3 c. water

Mix dry and wet ingredients separately, then combine together. Roll out 1/8" thick onto an oiled cookie sheet. Score. Bake at 325° for 25-30 min.

WHOLE WHEAT CRACKERS

1½ c. whole wheat flour	2 T. oil
1/4 t. salt	4 T. water

Combine dry and wet ingredients separately then mix together thoroughly. Roll out on an oiled cookie sheet. Score. Bake at 325° for 20-30 min.

EASY OAT CRACKERS

1¼ c. quick or rolled oats	1/4 t. salt
1/3 c. coconut	1/3 c. cold water
1 T. whole wheat flour	

Blend until fine oats and coconut. Pour into mixing bowl with flour and salt. Mix. Add water. Mix well. Roll out on to an oiled cookie sheet 1/8" thick. Score. Bake at 350° for 15-20 min.

FRITOS

1½ c. cornmeal	1 t. salt
3 c. hot water	2 T. oil, optional

Italics indicate item in index

Combine all ingredients and pour onto 2 - 10 x 15 oiled
cookie sheets. Distribute evenly by shifting pan from
side to side. Bake at 350° for 20 min. Remove from
oven and score. Bake an additional 40 min. During this
time remove the golden brown crackers on the outside edge
of the batter. This will need to be done about every 5
min during the last 20 min. Otherwise crackers will burn

COCONUT STICKS

1½ c. whole wheat flour
1/2 c. oat flour
1 t. *sweetener*
1/2 t. heaping salt

2 T. coconut
1/4 c. *nuts* chopped, or *seed*
3/4 c. water

Measure out a scant 1/2 c. of oats. *Blend* smooth.
Remove from blender. *Blend* smooth nuts and coconut with
1/2 c. of the water. Mix flours and salt then add
remaining ingredients. Knead in bowl 1 min. Pinch off
1 Tab of dough. Roll between hands to make a stick 1/2"
in diameter, 2-3" long. Bake on an oiled cookie sheet at
350° for 20-25 min.

CHEWY BRAN MUFFINS

3 c. oat flour
3 c. *raw bran*
1 c. water
1/2 c. coconut

1/2 c. dried fruit, chopped
1/4 c. honey or molasses
1¼ t. salt

Blend dry rolled or thick oats in blender to make a flour
Mix together dry ingredients. Combine wet then add to
dry. Pack into oiled muffin tins using a spoon dipped in
water to press with. This will prevent sticking while
molding dough. Bake at 350° for 40 min. Makes 12.
Serve with a fruit sauce such as apple or pear sauce.
For granola sprinkle batter on a cookie sheet. Bake at
225° for about 2 hrs or until dry. Stir occasionally.

SOY CORN MUFFINS

2 c. *soaked soybeans*
2 c. water
2 T. *sweetener*

2 t. salt
1/4 c. quick or rolled oats
2 c. cornmeal

Blend smooth all but cornmeal. Stir in cornmeal. Fill

Italics indicate item in index

6

oiled muffin tins and bake at 375° for 45 min. Serve
hot. Makes 18.

Variations:
(1) Pour batter into an oiled 8 x 8 baking pan. Bake at
375° for 50 min.
(2) Pour into oiled, hot cast iron gem pans. (Heat
pans in oven until water spatters when sprinkled on.)
For pie shaped gem pan bake at 375° for 60 min. For
corncob shape bake at 375° for 45 min.
(3) Use rye or barley flour in place of cornmeal and
oats. Or use uncooked corn grits.
(4) Use garbanzos in place of soybeans.

DODGERS

2 c. cornmeal	1¼ c. hot water
1/2 c. *soaked soybeans*	1 t. salt

Blend smooth 3/4 c. of the water with the beans. Combine
all ingredients. Drop onto oiled cookie sheet by heaping
teaspoons. May leave in a mound or slightly flatten.
Bake at 350° for 50 min. Crusty on outside, soft inside.

CORN OAT CAKES

2 c. cornmeal	1/4 c. dried fruit, chopped
2 c. rolled or quick oats	1/4 c. chopped *nuts or seeds*
1 t. salt	1 T. *sweetener,* optional
2¼ c. hot water	

Mix all ingredients together. Let set 10 min. Drop
by 1/4 c. full. Flatten to 1/2" high. Bake at 350°
for 45 min. on an oiled cookie sheet. Makes 12.
Variations:
Add 1 T. orange peel. Try roasted sesame seeds. Leave
out fruit when serving with a vegetable meal.

Italics indicate item in index

B R E A D S
(Yeast)

TIPS FOR BAKING YEAST BREADS

I. Ingredients

A. Flour - The higher gluten content (or the
    protein portion) of hard spring or winter
    wheat flour, in comparison to soft wheat or
    pastry flour, is the best for baking bread.
    The gluten works together with the yeast to
    make a nicely raised loaf. A mixture of two
    or three flours is quite nutritious and may be
    used for variety. Most other whole grain
    flours have very little gluten in them therefore,
    they should be limited to about one fifth of the
    total flour in a recipe. Soy flour adds
    moisture to a loaf. Avoid mixing a large
    number of grains in one loaf as this is a com-
    plex mixture which renders digestion more
    difficult. Ideal is one to three types of
    grain. Keep flour in refrigerator or freezer
    for long storage.

B. Yeast - Baking yeast may be purchased pre-
    packaged in one tablespoon proportions. It
    may also be obtained by bulk in 1/4 to 1 pound
    packages or more. The savings of buying in
    bulk can be tremendous. Yeast should be
    stored in the refrigerator or freezer. It
    will remain fresh for months or even more than
    a year with proper storage. Freshness may be
    tested by adding room temperature yeast to
    warm water and an equal amount of sweetener
    or as the recipe calls for. If it bubbles and
    doubles in size within ten minutes the yeast
    is still active. Salt, fat and too much
    sweetener(as is needed for a sweet bread)
    retard the action of the yeast. These items
    should be added after the yeast has developed.

8

C. Sweetener - The main purpose of sweetening in bread is to feed or help develop the yeast. Honey, molasses, corn syrup, and sugar will all accomplish this. If one uses the same amount of one of these sweeteners and yeast (example: 1 T. sugar to 1 T. of yeast) it is generally accepted that the yeast will consume the re-fined sweetener. Fruit juice and fruit sauce may also be used to develop yeast.

D. Salt - 1 t. per 2½ - 3 cups of flour is suf-ficient. May be left out.

E. Fat - This helps provide tenderness and moist-ness. Bread can be quite acceptable without fat as long as flour is used sparingly. Stop adding flour when dough is still slightly sticky but can be kneaded. Soy flour or ground nuts add moistness.

F. Water Temperature - Yeast develops best if the water it is added to is 80-90°.

G. Room Temperature - At least 68°. If warmer then raising time will be shorter.

II. Combining Ingredients

A. Order - 1st step is to add sweetener to warm water then sprinkle yeast on top. After yeast has bubbled 5-10 minutes add salt, oil and wheat flour. Develop the gluten in the batter by beating or stirring 1-2 minutes before adding other flours which have little gluten.

B. Kneading - This developes more gluten. It is done by vigorous rolling, folding and pushing of the dough with the hands for about 5 minutes. To prevent dough from sticking to hands either moisten hands and kneading surface with a little water or lightly flour hands and kneading surface.

C. Raising - This helps to lighten the bread. After kneading cover the dough with a clean towel and let double in bulk. This takes 20–45 minutes. Then the dough is punched down and kneaded for 1–2 minutes. If the dough is allowed to raise 2 or 3 times before placing in the bread pan it will increase in lightness. Raising time shortens each time dough is allowed to raise.

D. Preparation of Pans - Pans are available which require no oiling such as T-Fal, Silverstone or Teflon. If pans need to be treated a thin coat of oil may be used. The best treatment for non-sticking is to combine, in a jar, equal amounts of oil and lecithin. Wipe or brush into pans.

E. Shaping into Pan - Press out dough either with a rolling pin or hands to remove air bubbles. Roll or form the dough into a smooth loaf. Tuck it in so that the edges touch the sides of the pan. Cover the pan with a towel. When dough is doubled in bulk and ready to bake a slight indentation made with the finger will remain rather than spring back. If in doubt it is better to be slightly under raised. Place pans in a preheated oven.

III. Baking, Eating and Storing

A. Time and Temperature - The temperature is usually 350°. Preheat oven at least 10 minutes before pans are ready to go in. The time depends on the size of the loaf. A 1 pound loaf can bake in 40–45 minutes. A 2 pound loaf 50 minutes.

B. Check for Doneness - Particulary if not using oil it is important not to over bake bread. This causes dryness. The bread is done if it slips easily from a properly treated pan and the hand can be placed on the bottom of the

loaf without burning. Remove bread from pans
immediately and place on racks to cool. May
cover with a towel.

C. Bagging and Storage - Let bread cool at least
3 hours before bagging. It should feel cool and
dry to the touch. Bread keeps several weeks
to a few months in the freezer, several days
in the refrigerator and a few days at room
temperature.

D. When to Eat - There are some volatile substances
left in the bread after the fermentation process
of the yeast takes place. This will evaporate
in 1-3 days. Yeast bread is much more healthful and digestable a few days after baking.
The conditioning of the crumb proceeds during
the first few days, making the bread easier to
cut.

TROUBLE SHOOTING FOR BAKING HOMEMADE BREADS

1. SOUR TASTE
    a. Water too warm
    b. Period of rising too long, especially in whole
        grain breads which will not rise as light as
        white breads.
    c. Temperature too high while rising.
    d. Poor yeast.

    e. Bagging up before bread has completely cooled.

2. DRY OR CRUMBLY
    a. Too much flour in dough
    b. Over-baking
    c. Using flour with low gluten content. Hard
        spring or winter wheat is best for baking.

3. HEAVINESS
    a. Unevenness of temperature while rising.
    b. Insufficient kneading.
    c. Old flour
    d. Old yeast

4. CRACKS IN CRUST
    a. Cooling in a draft
    b. Baking before sufficiently raised.
    c. Oven too hot at first.

5. TOO THICK A CRUST
    a. Oven too slow
    b. Baked too long
    c. Excess of salt

6. DARK PATCHES OR STREAK
    a. Poor materials.
    b. Shortening added to flour before liquid, thus allowing flour particles to become coated with fat before they had mixed evenly with the liquid.

7. SOGGINESS
    a. Too much liquid
    b. Insufficient baking
    c. Cooling in airtight container

8. ILL-SHAPED LOAF
    a. Not molded well originally.
    b. Too large a loaf for the pan.
    c. Rising period too long.
    d. Failure to rise to greatest size in oven.
    e. Loaves flat on top may result from inadequate kneading.

9. COURSE GRAIN
    a. Too high temperature during rising.
    b. Rising too long or proofing too long.
    c. Oven too cool at first.
    d. Pan too large for size of loaf.
    e. Too much liquid.

BASIC WHOLE WHEAT BREAD

1 c. warm water	1 t. salt
1 T. *sweetener*	1 T oil, optional
1 T. yeast	2½ c. whole wheat flour

Italics indicate item in index

12

Dissolve sweetener in water then stir in yeast. Let
stand until yeast begins to bubble, about 5-8 min. Stir
in oil, if using it, and salt. Add 1 c. of flour. Beat
vigorously about for 1 min. Add 1 c. more flour, mix
well. Add remaining flour gradually. Use only that
amount necessary to be able to handle the dough without
it sticking to the hands. Lightly flour table and knead
dough about 5 min. Add more flour if necessary. Place
dough in clean large bowl. Cover with a clean towel.
Let dough rise until double, 30-45 min (in warm place).
Punch down, knead briefly. Be sure to squeeze out all
air bubbles. Shape into loaf. Place in lighted oil pan.
Cover with a towel. Let rise until double in size,
taking about 30-40 min. Bake at 350° for 40-50 min, until
golden brown and the bread slips easily from the pan.
Cool on a rack. Be sure it is thoroughly cooled before
bagging. See *Tips on Bread Baking* for more detailed
instructions and ideal method of oiling pans.

Variation:
For a lighter loaf substitute ¼ c. of gluten flour for
¼ c. of the whole wheat flour. Gluten is the protein
portion extracted from the wheat.

DILLY BREAD

2 c. onions, chopped	4 t. salt
1/2 c. water	3 T. oil, optional
3 T. yeast	1/2 c. cornmeal
1 c. warm water	1/4 c. *yeast flakes*
1/4 c. *sweetener*	2 T. dill seed, *blended*
1 c. whole wheat flour	1 c. unbleached white flour
1 c. additional water	4-5 c. additional whole wheat flour

Saute onions in ½ c. water. Combine yeast, honey and
warm water, let stand until bubbles appear. Beat additional water and 2 c. flour vigorously 1 min. Add yeast
mixture to this and allow to rise until double. To this
add onions and remaining ingredients. Knead 5 min. Let
double in size, punch down and form into loaves. Place

Italics indicate item in index

in 3 oiled pans. Let double in pans. Bake at 350° for
45-50 min.

ZWIEBACK

This "twice baked" bread is easier for digestion than if
bread were not toasted at all. Use any kind of yeast
bread except cracked wheat. Lay bread slices on oven
rack. Bake at 200° for 1½-3 hours until crispy dry.
Some breads dry faster due to lightness or thinness.
Watch for burning. Or, the pilot light in a gas oven
may be sufficient to dry bread overnight.

Variation:
Croutons may be made the same way only cut in cubes
before drying.

DROP BISCUITS

1½ c. warm water	2/3 c. cornmeal
1 T. *sweetener*	1 t. salt
1 T. yeast	1/4 c. *nuts or seeds*
1 2/3 c. whole wheat flour	1/4 c. water

Combine first three ingredients. Let stand until
bubbles appear. *Blend* nuts and 1/4 c. water smooth.
Mix all ingredients together. Drop by spoonfulls on
an oiled cookie sheet. Let rise 20 min. Bake at 350°
for 30-40 min or until golden brown. Makes 12-14.

BASIC WHOLE WHEAT MUFFIN MIX

3 c. whole wheat flour	2 T. yeast
1/2 c. oat flour or	2 T. honey
unbleached white flour	1 t. salt
2 c. warm water	2 T. oil

Make oat flour by *blending* dry quick or rolled oats into
a flour. Mix, and let stand 5 min, the water, yeast and
honey. Stir in remaining ingredients. Oil muffin tins.
Fill 1/2 full with batter. Or drop by large spoonfulls
on an oiled cookie sheet. Let rise 10-15 min. Bake at
350° for 30-35 min. Makes 18. Or place in an oiled
8 x 8 cake pan, let rise about 15 min. or until almost
double in bulk. Bake 45-50 min.

Italics indicate item in index

14

Variations:
Use the basic whole wheat muffin mix just as it is along with any of these variations (additions). When recipe reads to leave out certain items this pertains to the basic mix.

Soy, Millet or Buckwheat
1/2 c. flour from title   (leave out oat flour)

Raisin Orange
3/4 c. raisins   1 T. dried orange peel

Date Bran
3/4 c. bran   2/3 c. dates
(Leave out 1/4 c. whole wheat flour)

Blueberry
1½ c. berries   3 T. *sweetener*
1 t. vanilla   (leave out ½ c. water)

Pineapple
1-20 oz can crushed pineapple, well drained
1 t. vanilla   2 T. *sweetener*
(leave out ½ c. water)

Banana Nut
2 c. mashed banana   1/2 c. chopped *nuts or seeds*
(leave out 2/3 c. water)

Jam
3/4 c. dried fruit jam
After filling muffin tins drop 3/4 - 1 t. of jam on top of batter then let rise 10 min.

Cornbread
1 3/4 c. cornmeal   1¼ c. white four
(leave out oat flour and 2½ c. of the whole wheat)

Barley, Rice or Oat
1 c. flour from title
(leave out oat flour and 1/2 c. of whole wheat)

Italics indicate item in index

Carrot, Zucchini or Apple
2 T. honey (additional to 1½ c. carrot, zucchini or
    basic recipe)   apple, grated
1/2 c. chopped *nuts or seeds*(leave out ¼ c. water for the
1 T. coriander   carrot and ½ c. water for the
1 T. dried orange peel   apple and zucchini muffins)
1 t. vanilla
(leave out ¼-½ c. of the water depending on which fruit
or vegetable is being used.)

Carob
1/3 c. *carob*   2 T. honey (additional to
(Leave out ¼ c. water)   basic recipe)

Cheese
2 c. *cashew pimento cheese sauce*
(leave out 2/3 c. water)

Caraway Rye
1 c. rye flour   1½ t. caraway seed
                2 T. molasses
(leave out 1/2 c. whole wheat and all of oat flour,
also the honey)

BREAKFASTS

COOKING CHART FOR WHOLE GRAINS

Grain (1 cup)	Water (in cups)	Time

1. Rolled or Flaked:
   i.e. oats, barley, rice, rye
   soy, triticale,millet, wheat
	2-2½	1 hr.

2. Meal:
   i.e. cornmeal or *blended*
   millet
	2½	1½ hr.

3. Hulled:
   i.e., millet, rice, barley
   corn or soy grits
   cracked wheat, buckwheat
   oat groats, steel cut oats
	3	2 hr.

Italics indicate item in index

Grain (1 cup)	Water (in Cups)	Time
4. Whole berries:	3	3-4 hrs
i.e. wheat, rye, barley, triticale		

Crockpot - All cereals, except quick or rolled oats, do well in a crockpot overnight. Try mixing 2 or 3 for variety in texture and a unique taste. The temperature setting varies with different pots. The cereals needs to come to a simmer or light boil.

Salt - For each cup of water use ¼ t. of salt.

Cooking Directions - Bring water and salt to a boil in a covered sauce pan. Stir in grain, cover, and return to a boil. Turn heat down to a simmer and cook for recommended length of time. Do not stir grain after mixing with boiling water. Corn and millet meal will lump when added to boiling water unless 1 c. of water is left cold to stir with the 1 c. of grain before adding to boiling water.

Variations:
Ways to shorten cooking time:
1. Soaking grains overnight will save about 10 min for each hour of cooking.

2. *Dextrinizing* or toasting grains before adding water helps to break down raw starch grains. Large quantities of grains may be dextrinized ahead of time and stored the same as those not yet toasted. See *Chart for Dextrinizing Whole Grains.*

CHART FOR DEXTRINIZING WHOLE GRAINS

Dextrinization may be done in the oven or on top of the stove. No water is involved, only dry heat. Stir cereals in the oven occasionally. Grains on the stove need almost constant stirring. Use a cookie sheet in the oven and a large flat bottom pan, such as a skillet for the stove. Grains should take on a light golden brown.

Italics indicate item in index

Oven temperature should be 250°. Stove top medium low heat.

Grain	Dextrinizing: Oven	Stove (in min)	Add to Boiling Water and Cook(in m
Rolled or			
Flaked	30	12-15	20
Meal	45	12-15	30
Hulled	45	12-15	60

CORN MILLET PORRIDGE
1/2 c. millet
1/2 c. cornmeal
3 1/2 c. water, boiling
1/2 c. water, cool

1 t. salt
1/2 c. coconut
1/2 c. dates, chopped

Mix cornmeal in cool water, then add with millet into boiling, salted water. Also stir in coconut and dates. Cover and simmer 2 hrs.

FRUITED GRITS
3 c. corn grits, hot cooked
2 c. fruit, fresh, canned or frozen, drained
1/4 c. chopped *nuts or seeds*
coconut

See *Cooking Time Chart for Cereal* to properly cook grits. Mix all ingredients, pour into a serving dish. Sprinkle with coconut or more chopped nuts and serve immediately. Fruit may be warmed ahead of time.

Variation:
Use rice, millet or steel cut oats in place of grits.

SPROUTED CEREAL
1 c. whole grain *sprouts*
1½ c. rolled or flaked
   cereal, i.e. oats

3 c. water
3/4 t. salt

Bring water to a boil. Add salt and cereal. Simmer 30 min. Uncover and sprinkle sprouts around on top,

Italics indicate item in index

do not stir. Cover and continue to simmer 30 min.
Stir together before serving. Serve with fruit sauce,
Fruit Cream, or *Milk*

CAROB CRACKED WHEAT
6 c. water, boiling   2/3 c. dates, chopped
1½ t. salt   1/4 c. *carob*
2 c. cracked wheat

Stir all but dates into boiling water, cover. Simmer 2 hrs.
Stir in dates at end of the cooking.

WHOLE BERRY CROCK CEREAL
1 c. *berries*(barley, wheat, or rye)
1/2 c. millet or rice
4½ c. very hot tap water
1¼ t. salt

Combine all in the crockpot and let simmer overnight.
Some crockpots can accomplish this on Low or Medium but
there are some that must be on High to cook the grain so
that the shell bursts.

Variations:
    Choose 1 or 2. Stir in 20-40 min before serving.

1. 1/4 c. carob   3. 3/4 c. dried fruit,
2. 2 c. applesauce   chopped
4. 1/4 c. peanut butter of 1/3 c. *homemade nut or seed*
    butter.

GLORIFIED RICE
3 c. rice, cooked   1/2 c. chopped *nuts or seeds*
3/4 c. additional cooked   1/2 c. dried fruit, chopped
   cereal   1 c. crushed pineapple
1 c. pineapple juice
1/4 t. salt

Blend juice with additional cereal (may be rice or any
other kind). Stir all together and chill to serve.

    Italics indicate item in index

Variation:
Omit pineapple items and use apple juice and shredded apples or orange juice and fresh orange pieces.

BAKED OATS

2½ c. hot water	2 c. quick or rolled oats
1/2 t. heaping, salt	

Dissolve salt in water. Pour into 1 qt. flat baking dish. Sprinkle oats into water, stirring as little as possible. Bake, uncovered, at 350° for 50 min.

THREE GRAIN BAKE

1 c. quick or rolled oats	3 3/4 c. hot water
1 c. rolled barley	2 apples, chopped or
1 c. rolled wheat	shredded
1¼ t. salt	1/2 c. dried fruit, chopped

Dissolve salt in water. Pour into 2 qt. casserole. Stir cereals together and sprinkle into water. Drop fruit by hand into the cereal. Gently pat fruit in rather than stirring in. Over stirring can make cereal mushy. Bake at 350° covered for 40 min. Remove cover and bake an additional 10 min.

Variations:
1. Substitute any other type of rolled or flaked grain for the ones listed or just use one.
2. Use another type of fruit instead of apples (i.e. bananas)
3. Add 1/4 c. chopped nuts

MILLET RAISIN BAKE

2 c. *soaked soybeans*	3/4 c. raisins
1 c. millet, uncooked	1 c. water
2 c. pineapple juice	1¼ t. salt
1 T. *sweetening*	
1 20 oz. can crushed or chunk pineapple	
3/4 c. coconut	

Italics indicate item in index

Blend smooth beans and juice. Stir all ingredients together. Bake in an oiled 2 qt. casserole dish, covered at 375° for 1¼ hours. Serve with *milk* or fruit sauce.

Variations:
1. Use any other unsweetened fruit juice.
2. Use other kinds of dried fruit.
3. Use 3 c. of fresh, frozen or canned fruit for pineapple.

LEFTOVER CEREAL DELIGHT

2 c. leftover cooked cereal	1/2 c. chopped dried fruit
2 c. bread or *waffle* crumbs	or 1 c. fresh, frozen or
2 c. *milk* or juice	canned fruit
	1/4 c. coconut

Combine cereal, bread crumbs and milk. Put half on the bottom of a 1 qt. casserole. Follow with fruit then remaining cereal mixture. Top with coconut. Cover and bake at 350° for 35 min. Serve with additional *milk* or fruit.

BRANY GRANOLA

10 c. quick or rolled oats	1 T. salt
2 c. *raw bran*	1/4 c. *sweetener*
1 c. chopped *nuts or seeds*	1 c. water
1/3 c. oil	1 c. chopped dried fruit

Combine oil, water, sweetener and salt. Stir this into the oats, bran and nuts, stirring only enough to moisten dry ingredients. Spread out on cookie sheets and bake at 250° for 2-3 hours, until dry, stirring every 20-30 min. Add fruit after baking.

PEANUT BUTTER GRANOLA

6 c. quick or rolled oats	1/3 c. honey
1 c. flour	1/2 c. peanut butter
1/3 c. water	1 t. salt

Stir together well all but oats and flour. Add oats and flour stirring only enough to moisten the dry ingredients. Spread out on 1 or 2 cookie sheets. Bake at 250° for 2-3 hours, until dry. Stir every 20-30 min.

Italics indicate item in index

NUTTY GRANOLA
10 c. rolled or quick oats   1 c. additional *nuts or see(*
1 c. *nuts or seeds,* chopped   1/4 c. *sweetener*
1 T. salt   2/3 c. dried fruit, optiona]
1½ c. water

Mix oats, chopped nuts and salt. *Blend* smooth remaining
ingredients except the fruit. Pour into oats. Stir
only enough to moisten the oats. Spread on cookie
sheets. Bake at 250° about 2 hours, or until dry.
Stir every 20 min. Mix in fruit after baking.

MUESLI
2 c. *granola*   1/4 c. dried fruit, chopped
2 c. apples, chopped   3 c. *nut* or *soy milk* or
1/4 c. chopped *nuts or seeds*   fruit juice

Combine all ingredients. Let soak in the refrigerator
several hours before serving.

SWISS STYLE GRANOLA
4 c. fruit sauce, i.e. apple, plum
4 c. *granola*

Mix sauce and granola. Let sit overnight. Serve
cold or heat in oven at 350° for 30 min. Serve plain
or with one of the *milks*.

HOT GRANOLA
1 c. *granola*
2½ c. fruit juice i.e. apple, pineapple, grape

Bring juice to a boil in a covered sauce pan, add
granola, covered and simmer 15 min.

COBBLER
8 c. fruit, fresh, frozen or canned (drained)
1 c. juice or water   1 recipe *Drop Biscuits*
1½ T. cornstarch   2 T. *sweetener*

Dissolve cornstarch and sweetener in juice then mix

Italics indicate item in index

with fruit. Pour into an 11 x 7 baking dish. This
should fill pan about half full. Mix up the biscuits
and drop by tablespoons on top of the fruit. Leave
an inch between each spoonful. Let raise 15 min. Bake
at 350° for 40 min.

CRISP # 1

5 c . unbaked *Nutty Granola*   1 c. juice from drained
8 c. fruit, sliced (fresh   fruit or water
     frozen, canned-drained)   1 T. cornstarch
     if using berries leave   2 T. *sweetener*, optional
     whole

Dissolve starch and sweetener into juice. Add this
with the fruit to a 7 x 11 casserole. Top with granola.
Bake at 350° for 45 min. Serve plain or with *milk*.
Hot or cold. Fruit or combination of fruits to try
may include sliced apples, peaches, pears, plums,
pineapple chunks, strawberries, cherries, blueberries,
bananas or raspberries.

CRISP # 2

3 T. *sweetener*   ½ t. coriander, optional
3 T. oil   1 t. vanilla
1/3 c. water   ½ c. flour
1/2 t. salt   3 c. quick or rolled oats

Stir together all but flour and oats, then combine all
ingredients. Follow the directions in *Crisp #1* concerning the amount of fruit to use and remaining
instructions.

BREAD PUDDING

3 c. bread cubes, ¼-½"   1/2 c. *dried fruit jam*
3 c. apples, shredded or   2 T. peanut butter
     chopped, or other
     fruit

Stir together jam and butter. Combine all ingredients
and place in a 1½ qt., covered, casserole. Bake at
350° for 35 min or until fruit is soft. Serve plain
or with *milk.*

Italics indicate item in index

SALTY OIL-FREE POPCORN

When using an air popper have a spray bottle (i.e. Windex
filled with salted water (1 c. water and 2½ T salt). As
corn pops to the top of the popper spray it lightly. Be
careful not to soak the popped kernals. The hot air will
evaporate the water. Shake the bottle frequently during
use. This method is very acceptable but by further heatin
the popcorn will be very crispy. (1) put corn on a cooki
sheet and heat in a hot oven for a few min. Watch for
burning. Or (2) dry in microwave for 1 min, stir, then
heat 20 sec. more.

DIXIE TOAST

2 large bananas	1 t. salt
1/2 c. *nuts or seeds*	1 t. coriander
1½ c. water	1/2 t. orange extract
1 t. vanilla	

Blend smooth all ingredients. Coat both sides of bread
slices using a spatula. This will cover about 16 slices
of bread.

Method #1 - Frying - Use a non-stick skillet on medium
              heat. Brown on each side.
Method #2 - Broiling - Place on oiled cookie sheet
              and brown on each side.
Method #3 - Baking - Place on oiled cookie sheet.
              Bake at 350° for 20-30 min or when golden
              brown on bottom. Flip and bake an addi-
              tional 10-15 min.

For suggested toppings see *Waffle Tips - Ways to Serve.*

FRENCH TOAST

1 c. quick or rolled oats	1 t. salt
1/3 c. *nuts or seeds*	2 T. *sweetener*, optional
1 3/4 c. water	

Blend Smooth all ingredients. Follow spreading directions and choose one of the cooking methods outlined
under *Dixie Toast*. For suggested toppings see *Waffle
Tips - Ways to Serve.*

Italics indicate item in index

WAFFLE TIPS

1. Conditioning Waffle Iron - Irons with non-stick surfaces should only need oiled after being washed. Grids without this special surface generally need treated every 2 or 3 waffles. Condition grids when cold. Lightly brush with oil or vegetable shortening. A very good substance can be made from mixing together equal portions of oil and lecithin. Store in a jar.

2. Large quantities of beans and grains may be soak ahead, drained and frozen.

3. Baking Time - 6 inch irons bake in 8-10 min. 9 inch irons take 15-20 min. Longer baking (20 min) is preferred to help insure breakdown of raw starches.

4. Storage - Stack cooled, leftover waffles in a plastic bag and freeze.

5. Reheating - (A) For crisp waffles: (1) in the toaster; (2) on a cookie sheet for 5-10 min at 350°, or under the boiler.
   (B) For soft waffles: (1) Place in a covered casserole for 10-15 min at 350°; (2) Cover and place in microwave on high for 1 min.

6. Ways to Serve - Top with (a) *Apple Syrup;* (2) *Carob Millet Sauce;* (3) *Millet Pudding;* (4) *Ice Cream,* (5) *Fruit Cream,* (6) *Fruit Soup,* (7) apple sauce or other fruit sauce; (8) canned or frozen fruit, drained. Then thicken juice. 1 c. juice: 1½ T. cornstarch. In place of butter use: (1) *Homemade Nut Butter,* (2) *Emulsified Peanut Butter,* (3) *Better Butter,* (4) *Millet Butter* (5) *Tahini.*

7. Other uses for waffles - (1) bread for yeast-free or wheat-free or gluten-free diets; (2) bread crumbs; (3) *Zwieback;* (4) *Waffle Cake.*

Italics indicate item in index

25

BASIC OAT WAFFLE

2 c. quick or rolled oats   1/2 t. salt
2 c. water

Blend smooth all ingredients. Pour into hot waffle iron. Bake 15-20 min. Makes 2. See *Waffle Tips* for how to condition iron and ways to serve.

Variation:
Substitute 1/2 c. of the oats for another whole grain.

BASIC SOY OAT WAFFLE

1 c. *soaked soybeans*   2¼ c. water
1½ c. quick or rolled oats   1/2 t. salt

Blend smooth all ingredients. Pour into a hot waffle iron. Bake 20 min for a 9" iron. Makes 2. *See Waffle Tips* for how to condition iron and ways to serve.

Variations:
1. Substitute any dried bean or pea for soybeans. esp. garbanzos and navy beans.
2. Substitute any other whole grain for ½ c. of the oats, i.e., cornmeal, rye, barley,rice or millet.
3. Substitute *soy* or *nut milk* for the water.

BASIC NUT OAT WAFFLE

2 c. quick or rolled oats   1/2 t. salt
2½ c. water   1 t. vanilla
3 T. pecans   1 T. *Sweetener*

Blend smooth all ingredients. Pour into hot waffle iron. Bake 15-20 min. Makes 2. See *Waffle Tips* for how to condition iron and ways to serve.

Variations:
1. Substitute soy milk for water.
2. Substitute any other *nut or seed* for pecans.
3. Substitute ½ t. maple or walnut flavoring for vanilla.

Italics indicate item in index

BASIC WHOLE BERRY WAFFLE
2 c. soaked berries   1 T. *nuts or seeds*
    (wheat, rye, barley)   1/2 t. salt
2 c. water

Soak 1¼ c. of *berries* overnight. Drain. Reserve water
to make the 2 c. needed in the recipe. *Blend* smooth all
of the ingredients. Pour into hot iron. Bake 20 min.
Makes 2. See *Waffle Tips* for how to condition iron and
ways to serve.

BASIC CEREAL WAFFLE
3 c. leftover cooked cereal (millet, rice, barley ...)

Spread cereal with a spatula into a hot iron. Bake 15-20
min. Makes 2. See *Waffle Tips* for how to condition iron
and ways to serve.

APPLE ICING BREAD
1 recipe for *Basic Whole Wheat dough*
3 c. of apple or other fruit sauce   1/4 c. coconut
1/2 c. chopped dried fruit   1/4 c. chopped
                                       nuts or seeds

Roll out dough 1/4" thick onto an oiled cookie sheet.
Prick dough in 4 or 6 places with a fork. Let raise
10 min. Cover with fruit sauce then evenly sprinkle
remaining items on top. Bake at 350° for 35-40 min.

Variations:
1. Leave out nuts and seeds and spread a thin layer of
   emulsified peanut butter or *Homemade Nut Butter* on
   the dough before the fruit sauce.
2. Slice 2 bananas on the dough before the fruit sauce.

Italics indicate item in index

CHEESE AND MILK SUBSTITUTES

SOY MILK

1/2 c. *soy base*
1/3 c. cashews, rinsed
1/2 c. water
1 t. vanilla

2 T. *sweetener*
1/4 t. salt
4 c. additional water, cc

Blend smooth all but additional water. When smooth add remaining water. Chill. Shake before pouring.

Variations:
1. Add 2 c. of fresh, canned or frozen, (drained) fruit to the recipe, i.e., bananas, apples, oranges, strawberries. Choose 1 or 2 fruits.
2. Add 1 c. of dried fruit. This should first be soften 5 min in 1 c. of hot water from the recipe, i.e., apricots, pineapple, prunes.
3. Add 1/2 c. frozen juice concentrate.

NUT MILK

1 c. *nuts or seeds*
1 c. hot water
2 T. *sweetener*

1 t. vanilla
1/4 t. salt
3 c. additional water, col

Blend smooth nuts and hot water. Add remaining ingredients and *blend*.

LEMON COCONUT MILK

1/2 c. coconut
1/2 c. leftover cooked cereal
1½ c. pineapple juice
1/2 t. salt

1/2 t. lemon extract
1 c. water
1/2 c. additional water

Blend smooth all but juice and additional water. When smooth add remaining liquid.

Italics indicate item in index

CAROB MILK

1/2 c. *soybase*	3 T. *sweetener*
1/4 c. cashews, rinsed	1/4 t. salt
1 t. vanilla	3 c. water
3 T. *carob*	

Blend smooth all but 2½ c. water. Add remaining water after ingredients are smooth.

CREAMY MILK

2/3 c. leftover cooked cereal	1/2 t. salt
1/3 c. *nuts or seeds*	1 c. water, boiling
1/4 c. dates	2 c. additional water

Pour boiling water over dates. Let stand 5 min. *Blend* smooth all except additional water. Add remaining water when ingredients are smooth.

Variations:
2 T. of *sweetener* may be substituted for the dates.

FRUIT CREAM
1 c. fruit juice, i.e., pineapple or apple
1/2 c. left over cooked cereal
1 T. *nuts or seeds*

Blend smooth using 1/2 c. juice. When smooth add remaining juice. Use over cereal, fruit crisp, waffles, french toast or as a dressing for fruit salad.

CASHEW PIMENTO CHEESE SAUCE

1 c. water	1/3 c. pimento
1/2 c. sesame seeds	1 t. salt
1/2 c. cashews, rinsed	1 t. onion powder
1/4 c. *yeast flakes*	1/4 t. garlic powder
1/4 c. lemon juice	

Blend smooth all except lemon juice. When ingredients are smooth add juice to blender. Chilling will make sauce slightly thicker. Use as a dressing for salads or cooked vegetables, over pizza or lasagna, or on patties. See *variations* on nest page.
Italics indicate item in index

Variations:
(1) If avoiding night shades substitute 2/3 c. cooked
     carrots for pimento.   (2) For thin slices; pour
sauce onto oiled cookie sheet, 1/4" thick.   Bake at 350°
for 30 min.   (3) For thick slices: pour into an oiled
loaf pan 1" thick.   Bake at 350° for 30-35 min.   Chill
then remove from pan and slice.   This is rather soft.
(4) For more economical sauce substitute 1/2 c. hot
cooked millet or rice for the cashews.   Replace the
water and pimento with 1¼ c. stewed tomatoes with juice.
Chill in order for the hot cereal to cool and thicken.
(5) Substitute sunflower seeds for cashews or sesame
seeds or both.

GOLDEN SAUCE
3/4 c. potato, cooked   1 t. salt
1/2 c. carrot, cooked   2 T. lemon juice
1 1/3 c. water   2 T. *yeast flakes*
2 T. *nuts or seeds*

Blend smooth all ingredients.   Heat and serve over
vegetables, rice, pasta, as an open face sandwich.

CASHEW CHEESE SPREAD
1/3 c. rolled or quick oats   1 t. onion powder
1/2 c. water   1/2 t. garlic powder
1/2 c. pimento   3 T. *yeast flakes*
1/4 c. cashews, rinsed   1/3 c. lemon juice
1 t. salt

Blend oats to make flour.   Dextrinize oat flour in a
dry skillet at med. heat for 10 min. until golden brown.
Stir frequently.   *Blend* smooth flour with all but the
lemon juice.   Add juice to blender when ingredients
are smooth.   Pour into a sauce pan and simmer, stirring
frequently about 5 min.   Use on bread, crackers or as a
vegetable dip.

Italics indicate item in index

TOFU CHEESE SPREAD

1/2 c. water	3 T. lemon juice
1 T. tapioca	1/8 t. dill weed or seed
1/2 *lb. tofu*	1/2 t. onion powder
1/4 c. cashews, rinsed	1/4 t. garlic powder
3 T. pimento	3/4 t. salt

Blend smooth all ingredients. Cook over medium low heat, constantly stirring, 5-10 min or until tapioca is clear. Chill. Use as spread or dip.

AGAR CHEESE

3 T. pimento	1/2 t. salt
1/4 c. lemon juice	1/2 t. onion powder
2 T. cashews, rinsed	1/8 t. garlic powder
2 T. sesame seeds	1 c. water
3 T. *yeast flakes*	1 T. *Agar Flakes*

Lightly boil Agar and water together until clear, about 5 min. While cooking *blend* smooth remaining ingredients. Stir all ingredients together. Chill. This cheese is soft yet firm and gives a slight melting effect. Good for *grilled cheese*.

NUT CHEESE

1¼ c. *soaked garbanzos*	1/3 c. lemon juice
1 c. water	1 sm. onion, quartered
1/2 c. stewed tomatoes	1 clove garlic
or juice	1/4 t. sage
1/3 c. *nuts or seeds*	1 t. celery salt
1/3 c. *yeast flakes*	3/4 t. salt
3/4 c. cornmeal	1/3 c. olives, chopped,
	optional

Blend smooth all ingredients except the cornmeal and olives. Stir these into blended items. Pour into an oiled 1 qt. casserole. Cover. Bake at 350° for 60 min. Let cool in the dish. Slice. Serve hot or cold. Try with *Sun Spread, sprouts*, chopped tomatoes all inside Pita bread. Or cube and put in salads. Or in a tomato sauce for pizza, lasagna or vegetables. Or drop cubes in with green beans. Or as a stuffing for celery.

Italics indicate item in index

ORCHARD APPLE PIE

2 c. shredded raw apples   4 T. tapioca
2 c. pineapple juice

Soak tapioca in juice 5 min. Bring to a boil then simmer, stirring. Cook until tapioca is clear. Cool slightly then add apples. Chill. Pour into baked pie crust. Sprinkle with coconut or serve with *whipped cream.*

Variations:
1. Stir in 1/4 c. chopped dried fruit and 1/4 c. *nuts or seeds.*
2. Pie may be used as a main dish if using the *Oat-Fruit Pie Crust*

LEMON PIE

1/2 c. coconut, cashews   1/4 t. salt
     or almonds   1/4 c. cornstarch
1/2 c. water   2½ c. pineapple juice
3 T. lemon juice   2 T. *sweetener*
1/4 t. lemon extract

Bring pineapple and lemon juice to a boil. *Blend* smooth remaining ingredients. Stir blended ingredients into boiling juice. Simmer 10 min stirring until thickened. Pour into baked pie shell and chill. Sprinkle coconut on top or serve with *soy or cashew whipped cream.*

BERRY PIE

4 c. berries, any kind   1-4 T. *sweetener*, optional
2 c. fruit juice or water   1/8 t. salt
1/4 c. cornstarch

Cook until thick stirring, all but fruit. Let cool then add fruit. Pour into a baked pie shell. Chill.

Italics indicate item in index

DATE CREAM PIE

3/4 c. dates, chopped packed   1 t. dried orange peel
3 T. cornstarch   1/4 t. salt
1 c. *soymilk*, hot   1½ c. additional *soy milk*

Bring hot milk and dates to a boil, covered. Turn off heat and let stand 5 min. *Blend* smooth all ingredients. Pour into a saucepan. Cook until thick, stirring. Pour into baked pie shell or serve as a pudding. Chill.
Variation:
Try other dried fruits in place of dates.

PUMPKIN PIE

3 c. pumpkin or sweet potato, cooked and mashed
1/4 c. *sweetener*   1 t. orange peel
1 T. cornstarch   1 t. coriander
1/2 t. salt   2/3 c. cashews, rinsed
2 t. vanilla   1 c. of water

Blend smooth all but pumpkin or potato with 1/2 c. of the water. When smooth add remining liquid and as much of the pumpkin or potato as the blender can whiz. Pour contents, in with remaining squash. Stir well. Cook over medium heat in a sauce pan, stirring, for about 10 min. Pour into baked pie crust. Chill. To serve sprinkle coconut on top or top with *Cashew or Soy Whipped Cream.*

MILLET PUDDING

1 c. hot pineapple juice   2 T. cashews, rinsed
1 c. cooked millet, hot   1/8 t. salt
     packed   1 t. vanilla

Blend smooth all ingredients. Ways to serve: (1) sprinkle 1/4 - 1/2" of granola in bottom of a flat dish. Pour pudding over, 1-2" thick. Chill. Add fruit topping before serving. See this recipe under *Tofu Cheese Cake.*
(2) serve over waffles, french toast, or cereal. May stir in 1/2 - 1 c. fruit, i.e., drained pineapple chunks, banana slices, berries.

Italics indicate item in index

BANANA DATE PUDDING

1 c. dates, chopped & packed	1/4 t. salt
2 c. water, boiling	3 T. cornstarch
2/3 c. cashews or almonds	1 c. additional water
1½ t. vanilla	2 bananas, sliced

Pour boiling water over dates, cover. Let soften about 5 min then blend smooth. Empty into a sauce pan. *Blend* smooth remaining ingredients, stir into dates. Simmer until thick, stirring, about 10 min. Stir in sliced bananas. Pour into cups. Chill. Makes 4 cups.

Variation:
Add 1 T of cornstarch for a pie filling.
May use other varieties of fruits or nuts.

CAROB PUDDING

4 c. *soy or nut milk*	3 T. cornstarch
1/3 c. *sweetener*	1 t. vanilla
1/4 c. *carob*	1/2 t. salt

Stir or *blend* all ingredients until smooth. Pour into saucepan. Bring to a boil, stirring until thick, about 10 min. Pour into serving dish, cover and chill. Sprinkle with coconut before serving.

Variations:
To serve as a pie use 1/3 c. cornstarch

OIL-FREE PIE CRUSTS
See BREADS, Quick. Try the cracker recipes for *Easy Oat Crackers or Coconut Sticks*.
Oat-Fruit Pie Crust may also be used.

OAT-FRUIT PIE CRUST

1¼ c. oats	1/4 t. salt
1/2 c. apple sauce	

Mix together. Mold into an oiled pie dish, bake at 350° for about 25 min.

Italics indicate item in index

WHOLE WHEAT PIE CRUST

1 c. oat flour
1 c. whole wheat flour
1 t. salt

1/4 c. oil
1/2 c. water

Blend quick or rolled oats dry to make flour. Mix dry
and wet ingredients separately. Combine together,
stirring with a fork. Stir as little as possible.
Then, either press dough into an oiled pie pan by hand
or roll out dough then lay in pan. Bake 350°, 13 min.

Variation:
The *Whole Wheat Cracker* recipe could also be used.

CAROB MUFFINS OR CAKE

2 T. yeast
2 T. honey
2½ c. warm water
3 c. whole wheat flour
1/2 c. unbleached white
    flour or oat flour

1/2 c. *carob*
1/2 c. additional honey
1 t. salt
1 t. vanilla

Make oat flour by *blending* quick or rolled oats dry.
Mix together water, honey and yeast. Let sit 5 min.
Stir together all ingredients. Fill oiled muffin tins
2/3 full. Let rise 15 min. Bake at 400° for 20-30 min.
Makes 24 or two 8 x 8" cakes. Frost with *Coconut* or *Carob
Peanut Butter Frosting.*

FRUIT NUT CAKE

1/2 c. warm water
2 T. yeast
1 T. *sweetener*
1 1/3 c. mashed bananas
    (3 med size)
1/4 c. honey
1/2 c. chopped *nuts or seeds*

3/4 c. chopped dried fruit
1 t. vanilla
1½ t. salt
1 c. unbleached white flour
2 c. whole wheat flour

Mix together water, sweetener and yeast. Let sit 5 min.
Add to this all but 2 c. of flour. Stir flour in
gradually. Beat batter 1-2 mins. Place in an oiled

Italics indicate item in index

8 x 8" cake pan or in two 3 x 7" loaf pans. Let rise
40 min. Bake at 350° for 50 min. Top with frostings
or topping mentioned in this section.

WAFFLE CAKE

Make 4-9" waffles from any of the recipes mentioned in
this book.
Filling:
  1½ recipe of *Carob Pudding* with banana slices.
  1½ recipe of *Banana Date Pudding* with banana slices.
  1½ recipe of *Berry Pie* filling.
  2 recipes of *Orchard Apple Pie* filling.
  2 recipes of *Lemon Pie* filling with pineapple chunks
    or sliced grapes.
  2 recipes of *Date Cream Pie* filling with banana slice
  2½ recipes of *Millet Pudding* with sliced grapes or
    peaches, berries, pineapple chunks or banana
    slices. (Leave out ¼ c. of hot cereal with each
    recipe.)

Frost each waffle with about 1 c. of warm filling.
Stack one on top of another like a layer cake. On the
top waffle put 1½ c. of filling allowing it to drip over
sides. Chill remaining filling to frost sides just
before serving. Fruit should be layered on top of fillin
on each waffle. Insert tooth picks on top then cover wit
plastic wrap. Chill for at least 3 hours or overnight
before serving.
Serve as it is or with *Soy* or *Cashew Whipped Cream* or
with a little *Milk*. Serve as a main dish along with
Popcorn or as a dessert.

HARDY BANANA NUT CAKE

8-10 slices *zwieback* cubed	1 c. mashed bananas
2 c. fruit juice or water	1 T. dried orange or lemon peel
1/4 c. *sweetener*	2 c. flour
1 t. salt	1/4 c. *raw bran*
1 t. vanilla	¼-½ c. chopped *nuts or seed*
	1 t. coriander

Make ½" bread cubes before making them into zwieback.

Italics indicate item in index

Stir all ingredients together adding the cubes at end. Pack into an oiled 8" x 8" dish. Bake for 35 min. at 350°. Variation: Use 1 c. crushed pineapple or raisins for bananas. Top with frosting.

TOFU CHEESE CAKE

3/4 lb. of *Tofu*	1/2 c. *sweetener*
1 c. hot cooked millet or rice	1/4 c. lemon juice
	1 t. vanilla
1½ c. water	1/2 t. salt
2½ T. cornstarch	1/4 t. almond extract
1/2 c. cashews, rinsed	

Blend smooth all ingredients except tofu and 1/2 c. of the water. Pour this into a sauce pan. Add tofu and remaining water and *blend* smooth. Scrape into saucepan and cook, stirring, for about 10 min.

CRUST:
   2½ c. *granola* blended   5 T. water
   1½ t. coriander

Mix all ingredients together and pat down in an 8 x 8" casserole or baking dish. Pour tofu mixture over this and chill.

TOPPING:
   4 c. fruit, (fresh, frozen, canned-drained)
   2 c. fruit juice or water
   3 T. cornstarch
   1-3 T. *sweetener*, optional
   1/8 t. salt

Cook, stirring, all but fruit, 10 min. Let partially cool. Add fruit. Pour onto cheese cake and chill or spoon over as it is being served.

Italics indicate item in index

COCONUT VANILLA TOPPING

3/4 c. fruit juice	2 T. tapioca, quick
3/4 c. coconut	1/4 t. salt
1 t. vanilla	1½ c. additional juice

Blend smooth all but the additional juice. Gradually add this to the blender. Pour into a saucepan. Let sit 5 min then cook until tapioca is clear, stirring (about 10 min). Spoon over *Fruit Nut Cake, Banana Nut Cake, Waffles* or cereal. Or chill and use as an icing.

COCONUT FROSTING

1 c. water	3 T. *sweetener*
3/4 c. coconut	1/4 t. salt
1 T. cornstarch	1/2 t. extract (lemon orange, almond, etc.)

Blend until smooth all ingredients, cook until thick, stirring. Cool. Butterscotch flavoring is very good.

CAROB PEANUT BUTTER FROSTING

3/4 c. water, boiling	1/4 c. dates
1/2 c. peanut butter	1 t. vanilla
1/4 c. *carob*	1/8 t. salt

Pour boiling water over dates. Let sit 5 min. *Blend* smooth all ingredients. May also use as a spread. Chill.

CASHEW WHIPPED CREAM

1 c. water	1 t. vanilla
3/4 c. *Soy Milk Powder*	2 T. cashews, rinsed
2 T. *sweetener*	1 T. lemon juice

Blend until smooth all but lemon juice, stir this in at end. Chill. Makes 2 c.

SOY WHIPPED CREAM

2 T. water	1/8 t. salt
1/2 c. *soy base*	3/4 c. oil
2 T. *sweetener*	1 T. lemon juice
1 t. vanilla	

Italics indicate item in index

38

Blend all but oil and juice. Slowly pour in oil while still blending. Empty blender and gently stir in lemon juice. Chill.

CAROB BROWNIES

1/3 c. dates	1 t. salt
1/2 c. boiling water	1 t. vanilla
1/2 c. *soybase*	1 c. whole wheat flour
1/2 c. *sweetener*	1/2 c. nuts, chopped
1/2 c. *carob*	1/4 c. hydrogen perioxide
3 T. peanut butter	(H_2O_2)

Add dates to boiling water. Remove from heat. Let stand 5 min. *Blend* dates and water with all but last 3 ingredients. Pour into mixing bowl with flour and nuts. Preheat oven to 375°. Oil 8 x 8 baking dish. When oven is hot quickly stir in H_2O_2. Bake for 30 min. Top with *Carob Peanut Butter* or *Coconut Frosting*.

Variation:
Leave out H_2O_2 to make fudge.

NOTE: H_2O_2 should not be taken internally without first cooking. It is generally felt to be safe when exposed to heat for several min. It is made of oxygen and water and is very unstable. The initial bubbling acts as a leavening but quickly breaks down when exposed to air.

FUDGY CAROB BROWNIES

1 c. honey	1/3 c. oil
2 c. whole wheat flour	1½ t. *coffee substitute*
2/3 c. *soy* or *nut milk*	i.e. Pero
2/3 c. walnuts, chopped	1 t. salt
1/2 c. *carob*	1 t. vanilla

Stir until smooth all but the flour and nuts, stir them in last. Bake at 375°, in an oiled 8 x 8" pan, for 30 min. Top with *Carob Peanut Butter Frosting* when cool.

Italics indicate item in index

FRUIT BARS

1½ c. quick or rolled oats
1/2 c. millet flour
3/4 c. coconut

1/2 c. fruit juice,
(pineapple, apple or
orange)
1/4 t. salt

Millet flour can be purchased or simply add dry millet
to blender and *blend* until finely ground. Turn off
blender, bring up grain which is below the blade and
blend again. Mix all dry ingredients then add juice.
Stir only enough to moisten.

FILLING:
1½ c. of *Dried Fruit Jam* (i.e. pineapple, date or
a combination of 2 fruits.)

Put slightly more than half of the crumb mixture in an
oiled 5 x 7" baking dish, pat down. Spread filling over
this and top with remaining crust. Pat down. Bake at
350° for 40 min.

NUT BRITTLE

1 c. dates
2/3 c. water
1/2 c. cashews, rinsed

1 c. sesame seeds
1 c. coconut

Bring water to a boil. Add dates, cover, turn off heat.
Let sit 5 min. *Blend* dates, water and cashews smooth.
Mix together with coconut and sesame seeds. Bake in
oiled 8 x 8 baking dish, uncovered, at 350° for 30 min.
Cut in 1" squares and chill in refrigerator or freeze
and serve frozen.

Variations:
(1) Any dried fruit may be substituted for dates; (2)
Juice may be used for water. (3) Other nuts or seeds may
replace ones mentioned; (4) 1/2 c. of peanut butter
or other nut butter may replace cashews. (4) 1/4 c.
carob may also be stirred in.

Italics indicate item in index

COCONUT FRUIT BALLS

2/3 c. date butter
1 c. coconut
1/3 c. whole grain flour

1/4 c. quick or rolled oats
1/4 t. salt
1/3 c. peanut butter

See *Dried Fruit Jam* to make date butter. Mix dry
ingredients. Add wet. Shape into unshelled walnut
size balls. Place on oiled cookie sheet. Bake at 350°
for 35 min. Makes 14.

CAROB BALLS

1/2 c. *carob*
1/2 c. honey

1 c. peanut butter
coconut

Throughly mix carob into honey. Stir peanut butter into
this. Form unshelled walnut size balls by rolling between
palms. Roll in coconut. Freeze on a plate. Serve
frozen or cold. After frozen on a plate. Store in
plastic bag in the freezer.

FIG NEWTONS

Follow *Easy Oat Crackers* for the crust but adding 1 t. of
vanilla and 1 T. of *sweetener*. 1/3 c. of soy flour may
be substituted for 1/3 c. of the oats. This will give
a more golden color.
Filling: Make 1½ c. of fig jam following the directions
of *Dried Fruit Jam* using 1¼ c. chopped figs and 1 c. of
water or pineapple juice. Roll out dough 1/8" thick.
Cut stripes 3" x 6". Place filling 1" wide and 1/4"
thick down the center of the strip. Fold sides over
the filling. Place on an oiled cookie sheet, seam side
down. Bake at 350° for 20 min. Slice strips into 1½"
after cooled. Makes 18.

TAHINI COOKIES

6 T. *tahini*
3/4 c. honey
1/4 t. salt

1½ c. quick or rolled oats,
dextrinized
1/2 c. *nuts or seeds*

Mix dry and wet ingredients separately then all together,
let sit 10 min, bake on oiled cookie sheet at 350° for
10 min or until golden brown and slightly sticky.
Makes 12.

Italics indicate item in index

41

APPLE ORANGE COOKIES
1½ c. applesauce or mashed bananas
1 3/4 c. quick or rolled oats 1 t. dried orange peel
1/4 c. flour   1/2 t. salt
1/4 c. chopped *nuts or seeds* 1 t. vanilla
1/4 c. chopped dried fruit

Stir together dry ingredients then combine with remaining
items, stirring only enough to moisten oats. Shape
into cookies, ¼-½" thick. Bake on oiled cookie sheet
at 350° for 35 min. Makes 12 large cookies.

PEANUT BUTTER COOKIES
1/4 c. honey   1/4 c. water
2/3 c. peanut butter   1/4 t. salt
1 3/4 c. oat flour

Make oat flour by *blending* quick or rolled oats. Stir
together all ingredients, adding the flour last. Shape
into small balls the size of an unshelled walnut. Place
on an oiled cookie sheet. Flatten with a fork that is
moistened with water to about ¼" thick. Bake at
350° for 30 min, until golden brown. Makes 15-18.

GOLDEN MACAROONS
1 c. grated raw carrots,   2 c. coconut
  packed   1/4 c. soy or oat flour
1/4 c. water   1/4 c. whole wheat flour
1/3 c. honey   1/2 t. salt
1 t. almond or vanilla extract

Blend dry, quick or rolled oats to make a flour. Mix
well all ingredients. Let sit 10 min. Firmly pack
dough into a tablespoon then place on an oiled cookie
sheet. Bake at 325° for 30 min.

OATMEAL RAISIN COOKIES
1 c. honey   1½ c. whole wheat flour
3/4 c. water   1 t. vanilla
2/3 c. oil   1½ t. salt
1/2 c. raisins   1¼ t. lemon extract
1/2 c. chopped *nuts or seeds* 5 c. quick or rolled oats

Italics indicate item in index

42

Stir together all but oats. Gradually mix these in.
Let batter sit 10 min. Shape heaping tablespoon of
batter by hand. Place on oiled cookie sheet. Bake at
350° for 30-35 min. Makes 3-4 dozen.

Ice cream may be served alone or over *waffles, granola*
cooked cereal, *popcorn, muffins* or *french toast*. Use
sparingly. Warm in the mouth before swallowing as very
cold foods in the stomach slow digestion (this holds
true with very hot foods or drinks as well).
Champion Juicers make delicious soft serve ice cream
simply by running frozen fruit, alone, through the
machine.

BANANA ICE CREAM
4 bananas, frozen, cut into fourths. Blend with enough
soymilk to turn blades. About ¼ - ½ c. milk.

CAROB ICE CREAM
2 bananas peeled and frozen   1/4 c. *carob milk*

Break bananas into chunks. Drop in blender with milk.
Blend smooth. Add a little more milk if blades do not
turn. Return to freezer for up to 30 min or serve
immediately.

MAPLE WALNUT ICE CREAM
5 frozen bananas, chopped   1/2 t. vanilla
1/2 c. water   1/2 t. maple flavor extract
3 T. walnuts, or other   1/8 t. salt
    nuts or seeds

Blend smooth all but bananas. Slowly drop chunks of
banana in while blender is running. Add more water if
unable to blend all banana. Serve immediately or return
to freezer for up to 30 min before serving.

Variations:
1. Use 2¼ c. peaches plus 2 T of *sweetener* in place
    of bananas.
2. Substitute maple for butterscotch, walnut, or vanilla
    butter and nut flavoring.

Italics indicate item in index

BANANA BON BONS
Peel banana, cut in half crosswise then coat with one of the following:

1. *Dried Fruit Jam*
2. *Carob Peanut Butter Frosting*
3. *Emulsified Peanut Butter* or *Tahini*
4. *Homemade Nut* or *Seed Butter.*

Roll coated banana in coconut. Place cut side down on a plate and put in the freezer. When frozen serve as they are or for easier serving cut each section in half again and poke a toothpick in the center. Store left over bon bons in a plastic bag.

DRESSINGS, GRAVIES AND SPREADS

A big question is "How Long Do These Dressings and Spreads Keep?" Since they do not have preservatives in them naturally they don't keep as long but *much depends on you.* With proper attention these items should last 1½ - 2 weeks. (Ketchup and fruit spreads generally keep 2-3 weeks.) Keep item in the refrigerator as much as possible. This includes: (1) shortly after preparation; (2) not setting it on the table until it is time to eat; (3) put back in the refrigerator first thing after the meal (not after the dishes are done); (4) put in serving containers which will likely be empty after 3-5 meals. (5) do not mix a more fresh recipe in the same serving dish as one that has been exposed to room temperature several times; (6) do not use the same serving spoon on an older spread and a fresh spread as the old one runs out; (6) If amount is more than will likely be used in 2 weeks cut the recipe. Most of these do not freeze well. (The consistency is different after freezing).

Italics indicate item in index

SAVORY BOUQUET

1 c. water	1/2 c. *nuts or seeds*
3/4 t. salt	2 T. lemon juice
1/4 t. onion powder	1/8 t. garlic powder
1/8 t. thyme	1/2 t. sweet basil

Blend all in blender until smooth.

SUN SEED TOMATO DRESSING

1½ c. canned tomatoes with juice	1 t. *sweetening*
	1/8 t. garlic powder
1/2 c. sunflower seeds	1/2 t. onion powder
1/4 c. lemon juice	
3/4 t. salt	

Use half of the tomatoes to *blend* smooth remaining
ingredients. Then add to blender remaining tomatoes.
Use as a salad dressing.

HUMMUS

1 c. cooked garbanzo beans	1 clove garlic
1/4 c. sesame seeds, toasted	1/2 t. salt
3 T. lemon juice	1/2 c. water

Toast seeds in a dry skillet on medium heat about 5 min,
stirring frequently, until golden brown. *Blend* all
ingredients until smooth. Serve as a dressing or sandwich spread.
Variation: Substitute 1/4 c. *tahini* for the seeds.

LOW-CAL FRENCH DRESSING

1 c. cooked tomatoes	1/8 t. celery salt
1/4 t. onion powder	1/8 t. salt
2 T. lemon juice	1/8 t. garlic powder
1 t. *sweetener*	1/8 t. basil

Blend all ingredients.

Italics indicate item in index

SUMMER SALAD DRESSING
2 T. *nuts or seeds*
1 c. water
1/2 c. avocado, mashed
3-4 T. lemon juice

1/4 t. garlic powder
1¼ t. onion powder
3/4 t. salt

Blend smooth all ingredients.

CREAMY DELUXE DRESSING
1/2 c. *nuts or seeds*
1/8 t. garlic powder
1 t. onion powder
1/2 c. cooked cereal
2 c. tomatoes, canned
1 T. *sweetener*

1/2 t. salt
2 t. *Yeast Paste*
4 T. lemon juice
2 t. *yeast flakes*
1/8 t. basil

Blend smooth all ingredients.

FRENCH TOMATO DRESSING
1/2 c. oil
1/4 c. lemon juice
2 T. *sweetener*
1 t. paprika

3 T. tomato paste
1 t. salt
1/4 t. onion powder
3 T. water

Blend smooth all but oil and juice. While blender is still running slowly pour in oil. Remove from blender and stir in lemon juice.

SOY GARBANZO MAYONNAISE
1 c. *soybase*
1 c. cooked garbanzo beans
1 c. water
1/4 c. cashews, rinsed
1/4 c. sesame seeds

1/4 c. lemon juice
1½ t. salt
1 clove garlic
1/2 t. celery seed
1/2 t. onion powder

Blend all until smooth. See cooking instructions for beans to cook garbanzos. Use over salads, vegetables or breads. Try with *Potato Salad*.

Italics indicate item in index

SOY MAYONNAISE

1/2 c. *Soy Milk Powder*	1½ t. onion powder
3/4 c. water	2 T. lemon juice
3/4 t. salt	1/4 c. oil
1/8 t. garlic powder	

Blend smooth all ingredients except the oil and lemon juice. Continue blending and slowly pour oil in. Remove from blender and stir lemon juice in. Use in sandwiches, *Potato Salad* or add 1 T. of lemon juice to make sour cream.

SUN SEED SPREAD

1/2 c. sunflower seeds	1 t. salt
½ c. millet, or rice	1½ t. onion powder
cooked, hot	1/2 t. garlic powder
3/4 c. water	1/8 t. dill weed or seed
1/3 c. lemon juice	

Blend all until smooth. Serve on crackers, bread, as a vegetable dip or as a sour cream for baked potatoes.

YEASTY SPREAD

1/2 c. *Sun Seed Spread, Soy Garbanzo Mayonnaise or
        Soy Mayonnaise*
1/4 c. *Yeast Flakes*

Stir ingredients together well. Spread over bread or crackers, as a salad dip, or on baked potatoes.

BEAN SPREAD

1 c. cooked beans, salted	1/4 c. dressing

Mash or *blend* beans with the dressing of your choice. Try *Savory Bouquet, Soy Garbanzo Mayonnaise, Cashew Pimento Cheese Sauce, Ketchup, Golden Sauce* or *Creamy Deluxe Dressing.*

AVOCADO BUTTER

1 c. avocado, mashed	1 t. onion powder
2 T. lemon juice	1/2 t. garlic powder
3/4 t. salt	

Mix by hand or *blend* until smooth.

Italics indicate item in index

KETCHUP #1

6 oz. can of tomato
    paste
6 oz. water
2 T. lemon juice
1/4 t. salt

3/4 t. onion powder
1/4 t. basil
1/4 t. dill weed or seed
1/4 t. garlic powder

Mix well.

KETCHUP #2

1/2 c. tomato paste
2 T. lemon juice
1 T. *sweetener*
1/4 t. onion powder

1/4 t. salt
1/8 t. garlic powder
1/8 t. oregano

Mix together all ingredients.

BETTER BUTTER

3/4 c. cornmeal or grits,
    cooked, hot
1/2 c. water

1/4 c. coconut
1/2 t. salt

Blend until smooth. Use on bread and vegetables.
Does not melt.

Variation
1. Replace coconut with other *nuts or seeds*.
2. Add 1/4 t. maple flavor.

MILLET BUTTER

1 c. cooked millet, hot
1/3 c. coconut
1/4 c. carrots, cooked, opt.

1 c. water
3/4-1 t. salt

Blend until very smooth and chill. Carrots are just
for color. Add more water if necessary.

FRESH CORN BUTTER

1 c. fresh or frozen corn, cooked
1/3 t. salt
                     2 T. water

Blend all smooth. Serve over bread, corn on the cob or
other vegetables.

Italics indicate item in index

EMULSIFIED NUT BUTTER
1/2 c. commercial nut or seed butter i.e., peanut butter
    or *tahini*

1/4 c. water   1/4 c. additional water

Stir with a fork the nut butter and water. Mix well.
Add as much additional water as needed to make butter
creamy and easy to spread but not runny. May use juice
in place of water. Refrigerate.

NUT OR SEED BUTTER
1 c. *nuts or seeds*   1/4 t. salt

1/2 c. water   ¼-½ c. additional water

Blend smooth all but additional water. Add as much
from the additional water as need to turn blender blades.
Some nuts require more water than others. Refrigerate.

SESAME COCONUT SPREAD
1/2 c. sesame seeds   1/2 t. vanilla, optional

1/4 c. coconut   1/2 t. salt

1 T. *sweetener*   3/4 c. water

1/4 c. almonds

Blend all ingredients until smooth.

PEANUT PINEAPPLE JAM
1 c. peanut or other nut butter, emulsified. Mixed
with 1/2 c. crushed pineapple, drained. Refrigerate.

CAROB PEANUT BUTTER
2 bananas or 3/4 c.   1-2 T. *sweetener*, optional

   applesauce   1/2 c. peanut or other

1/2 t. vanilla, optional   nut butter

2 T. *carob*

Blend or stir until smooth.

DRIED FRUIT JAM
1 c. chopped dried fruit   3/4 c. water or fruit juice

Bring water to a boil in a covered sauce pan. Turn off
heat, Stir fruit in. Cover and let sit 5-10 min, until
soft enough to blend. *Blend* smooth. Add more water
if needed. See *Variations* on following page.

Italics indicate item in index

Variations:
1. Combine dates and apricots with pineapple juice.
2. Add ½ t. of dried orange or lemon rind to date jam.
3. Add ¼ c. shredded fresh apples, mashed banana or crushed pineapple to fig, peach, date, prune or apple dried fruit jam.
4. Combine any 1 or 2 dried fruits with water or apple, grape, orange or other juices.

AVOCADO PINEAPPLE SPREAD
avocado, mashed
banana, mashed

crushed pineapple,
    drained

Mix or *blend* equal amounts of each item.

APPLE BUTTER
1 qt. applesauce
1/2 t. vanilla

1/2 t. coriander

Mix all, pour into flat baking pan 1" deep. Bake at 350° for 1 hour, or until reaching desired consistency. Stir occasionally during baking.

STRAWBERRY JAM
1 c. strawberries
2-4 T. *sweetener*
1/2 t. vanilla

1 T. tapioca

Blend all until smooth, simmer until tapioca is clear, stirring frequently. Chill.

FRUIT SPREADS
1 c. fruit juice
1½ T. cornstarch or quick tapioca

Stir ingredients together in a sauce pan. If using tapioca allow ingredients to sit 5 min. Bring to a light boil, stirring. Turn down heat to a simmer continue to stir. Cook about 5-10 min until slightly thickened. Tapioca should be clear. Chill.

Variations:
Add ¼-½ c. fruit, drained. This may be crushed pineapple, diced peaches or bananas, shredded apples or other varieties of fresh, frozen or canned fruit.

Italics indicate item in index

APPLE SYRUP
2¼ c. apple juice or pineapple   1 T. lemon juice
2 T. cornstarch   1/2 t. coriander

Combine and bring to   boiling, stirring, then simmer.
Cook about 10 min. Serve warm over waffles, french toast,
cereal. It will thicken more as it chills.

BROWN GRAVY
1/2 small onion   1½ t. *Yeast Paste*
1/2 small potato, leftover   1½ T. flour
     or raw
1½ c. water
1½ t. *Beef* or *Chicken Style Seasoning*

Bring to boil 3/4 c. of the water. *Blend* smooth
remaining water with ingredients. While water is
boiling stir in blended portion. Simmer until thick,
stirring frequently.

BROWN RICE GRAVY
1 c. rice or millet, cooked   1/2 t. salt
1.4 c. *nuts or seeds*   2 c. water
2 t. *Chicken Style Seasoning*

Blend smooth all but 1 c. of water. Pour into a
saucepan. Rinse out blender with remaining water and
add to blended ingredients. Heat and serve.

Variation:
Substitute 3T. of peanut butter for nuts to make
Peanut Butter Gravy. Serve for breakfast over hot corn
grits.

CASHEW GRAVY
1/2 c. water   2 t. onion powder
1/4 c. cashews, rinsed   1/4 t. salt
2 T. cornstarch   1 3/4 c. additional water
2 T. *Soy Sauce*

Blend smooth all but additional water. Pour blended
ingredients into a sauce pan. Rinse blender with additional water and pour in pan. Cook, stirring, until
thickened (about 10 min.) Variations on next page.

Italics indicate item in index

Variations:
1. Substitute other *nuts or seeds* for cashews.
2. For an *Herb Gravy* add the following:
   3 T. *yeast flakes* 1/8 t. sage, ground,
   1/8 t. thyme, ground, 1/8 t. oregano, 1 clove of
   garlic. Soy sauce may be replaced by ½ t. of salt.

POTATO GRAVY

1½ c. potatoes, chopped cooked	1/2 t. garlic powder
2 c. water	1/2 t. salt
2 T. *Soy Sauce*	1/4 t. basil
1 t. onion powder	

Blend smooth all ingredients. Heat and serve.

ENTREES

ITALIAN MEAT BALLS

1½ c. whole wheat flour	1 T. basil
2 c. bread crumbs, *blended*	1 t. marjoram
2 T. parsley, dried	1 t. salt
2 c. *Cashew Pimento Sauce*	1/2 t. garlic powder
1 c. walnuts, ground	

Grind walnuts dry in blender. Stir together all
ingredients. Use as meatballs, patties or a loaf.

For *Meatballs*: Form balls by hand. Bake on oiled
cookie sheet 40 min. at 350°.

For *Patties*: Shape patties about ½" thick and 3" in
diameter. Bake on an oiled sheet at 350° for 45 min.

For *Loaf*: Pack into an oiled loaf pan and bake at
350° for 1¼ hr. or bake in an oiled 8 x 8" pan for
60 min, uncovered. Serve hot with gravy or cold in a
sandwich with *Ketchup* or *Cheese Sauce, Millet Butter*
and *Sprouts*. Leftovers freeze well. Good for sack
lunches.

Italics indicate item in index

52

PECAN LOAF

1/4 c. sunflower or sesame seeds	
2/3 c. flour	1½ t. salt
1 medium onion, quartered	1 c. pecans, ground
1½ c. water	2 c. brown rice, cooked
1 t. basil	4 c. bread crumbs, *blended*

Grind pecans dry in blender to make a meal. Remove from blender and mix together with rice and *blended* bread crumbs.

Blend remaining ingredients until smooth. Combine all. Use for meatballs, patties or as a loaf.

See *Italian Meatballs* for baking and serving instructions.

Variations: (1) Use cooked millet for all or part of rice. (2) Use other nuts or seeds for pecans and seeds.

MILLET PATTIES

3/4 c. flour	1 t. basil
2/3 c. *nuts or seeds*	1/2 t. sage or thyme
1 large onion, quartered	4 c. millet, cooked
1 c. water	2 c. bread crumbs, *blended*
1 t. salt	

Blend until smooth all but millet and *blended* bread crumbs. After blending mix all ingredients together.

See *Italian Meatballs* for baking and serving instructions. May use for meatballs, patties or as a loaf.

MILLET TOMATO LOAF

1 c. millet, uncooked	1/2 t. sage
1 c. tomato juice or stewed	1/2 t. savory or marjoram
tomatoes	3 c. additional tomato
1 medium onion, quartered	juice or blended tomato
1/4 c. cashews or almonds	1/2 c. olives, chopped,
1 t. salt	optional
¼ c. sesame seeds	

In a 2 qt. casserole combine additional juice or stewed tomatoes (*blended*), along with millet and olives. *Blend* smooth remaining ingredients. Stir into casserole. Cover and bake at 350° for 1 hr, and 20 min. Remove from oven, take lid off and let set 10 min before serving.

Italics indicate item in index

LENTIL NUT LOAF OR PATTIES

3 c. lentils, cooked dry	1 t. salt
1/2 c. chopped *nuts or seeds*	1/2 t. celery seed
1 T. onion powder	1/2 c. rolled or quick oats
1/4 t. sage	1/4 c. water

Mix all ingredients together. Place in an oiled loaf pan or casserole. Bake, uncovered at 350° for 60 min. Serve with gravy or *Ketchup*. Or chill and serve for sandwich slices. Bake patties 40 min.

Variation:
Other beans may be used in place of lentils.

OATBURGERS

1/4 c. sunflower seeds	1 t. oregano
1/4 c. *yeast flakes*	1 clove garlic
1 medium onion	1 c. water
2 t. salt	1/4 c. sesame seeds, toasted
1 T. basil	4½ c. quick or rolled oats
1½ t. dill seed	3 c. additional boiling water

Toast sesame seeds in a dry skillet over medium low heat, stirring, 5 min. Bring the 3 c. of additional water to a boil. While doing this *blend* smooth all except the oats and sesame seeds with the 1 c. of water. Mix all ingredients together into the boiling water continuing to stir for one minute. Remove from heat and let sit 15 minutes. Form into patties ½" thick. Place on oiled cookie sheet. Bake at 350° for 30 min, turn over and bake an additional 20-30 min. Makes 15-20. May freeze leftover patties.

GARBANZO RICE PATTIES

1¼ c. *soaked garbanzo beans*	2 t. *chicken style seasoning*
1½ c. rice, cooked	1/2 t. salt
3/4 c. water	1/2 t. onion powder
1/3 c. chopped *nuts or seeds*	1/8 t. garlic powder
3 T. *yeast flakes*	

Blend until fairly smooth beans and water. Mix all in a bowl, form into patties ½" thick, 3" in diameter. Bake on an oiled cookie sheet at 350° for 30 min, turn over and bake an additional 15 min. Makes 10-12.

Italics indicate item in index

SUN SEED ROAST

3/4 c. hot water
3 c. rolled or quick oats
3/4 c. sunflower seeds
1 c. onions, chopped

3 T. *Yeast Flakes*
1/3 t. thyme, ground
1 3/4 t. salt
3 c. hot water, additional

Blend smooth all but oats, onions and additional water.
Combine all ingredients, adding the oats last, stirring
them in gently and briefly into an oiled 2 qt. casserole.
Cover and bake at 350° for 45 min. Uncover and bake
15 additional minutes.

Variations:
1. Substitute barley or wheat flakes for oats.
2. Substitute walnuts or other *nuts or seeds* for
    sunflower seeds.
3. Chop nuts instead of blending.

GRILLED CHEESE

Spread a thin layer of *Millet Butter* or *Better Butter* on
both sides of bread slices. Lay on plate. Spread with
Agar Cheese ¼" thick. Add thin slice of onion and
tomato, if desired, then top with bread. Grill in non
stick pan on medium low heat until golden brown on each
side. 1 Agar Cheese recipe makes 8 sandwiches. Also
may broil open face sandwiches on a cookie sheet
following directions above.

PEANUT MEAT

1½ c. peanuts, dry roasted
2 c. water
1/2 c. cornmeal
1/3 c. soy flour or oat flour

1 t. salt
1 t. *Yeast Paste* or
   additional 1/3 t. salt

Blend peanuts with 1 c. water. Make oat flour by
blending quick or rolled oats. Stir all ingredients together. Bake, in oiled 1 qt. casserole, covered, at
350° for 60 min. Cool, remove from dish and slice.
Serve in sandwich with *Sprouts* and *Ketchup* or *Cheese
Sauce*. Cube and put in a salad. Use in *Peanut Rice
Casserole*.

Italics indicate item in index

PEANUT RICE CASSEROLE
4 c. cooked rice
1½ c. *Peanut Meal*

2 c. *Brown, Cashew* or *Brown Rice Gravy*

If rice and gravy are hot stir all ingredients and serve.
Or may be reheated, covered, in a 2 qt. casserole dish
at 350°.

SPANISH RICE
3 c. rice, cooked
1¼ c. stewed tomatoes
2/3 c. tomato paste
1 c. garbanzo beans,
    cooked, optional

1 c. onions, chopped
1 c. green pepper, chopped
1 t. basil
1/2 t. salt

Simmer, until vegetables are tender, all ingredients but
rice and beans. Add rice and beans. Simmer an additional
15 min or bake, uncovered, 45 min. at 350°. Baking
will help it to set more firmly.

CARROT RICE LOAF
2 c. rice, cooked
2 c. carrots, finely grated
1/2 c. bread crumbs
1/2 c. onions, chopped
1/4 c. peanut butter

2 c. *Soy* or *Nut Milk*
1½ t. salt
1 t. onion powder
1/2 t. garlic powder
1/4 t. thyme

Dissolve peanut butter into milk. Mix all ingredients
together. Bake in an oiled 2 qt. casserole, uncovered
at 350° for 45 min. If ingredients are cold add 15 min
to baking time. Serve plain or with *Brown Rice Gravy*.

GARBANZO NOODLE CASSEROLE
4 c. cooked whole grain noodles
1 c. cooked garbanzo beans
1½ c. *Brown* or *Cashew Gravy*

1/2 c. onion, chopped,
    cooked
1/2 c. celery, diced,
    cooked

Combine all ingredients. Bake at 350° in a covered
2 qt. casserole until hot or heat in a sauce pan to serve.

Italics indicate item in index

MACARONI AND CHEESE
3 c. cooked macaroni   1/4 c. onion, chopped, cooked
   (1 c. uncooked)   1/4 c. olives, chopped,
1 c. *Cashew Pimento Cheese*   optional
   Sauce
Heat in a sauce pan or in the oven, covered.

PIZZA
Crust:
   A double recipe of *whole wheat pie crust* or other
   recipes recommended for a crust. Or 1 recipe of
   Basic Whole Wheat Bread dough. Pie crusts should be
   1/8" thick. Roll out dough ¼" thick. Cover with
   sauce about ¼" thick.
Sauce:

4 c. stewed tomatoes	1 T. honey
1½ c. tomato paste	2 t. basil
1½ c. onions, chopped	3/4 t. salt
1/2 c. green pepper,	1/2 t. marjoram
chopped	1/2 t. oregano
1 T. lemon juice	1-2 cloves garlic, minced

Combine all ingredients. Bring to a boil and simmer
20 min and pour over crust. Bake at 350° for 30 min then
add Topping.
Topping:
   Evenly spread or drizzle in a criss cross design
   1-2 c. *Cashew Pimento Cheese Sauce*. Sprinkle with
   1/2 c. sliced olives. Continue to bake 15 min.

LASAGNA
1/2 lb whole grain noodles, (about 8-11")
1 recipe of *Pizza* sauce, hot   1/4 t. salt
1/2 lb *tofu*   1-2 c. *Cashew Pimento Cheese*
1/4 c. lemon juice   *Sauce or Agar Cheese*

Blend tofu, lemon juice and salt with just enough water
to turn blades. Cook noodles in boiling salted water.
Drain into a colander and rinse briefly with cold water.
Oil a 7 x 11 baking dish. Make a single layer of noodles,
side by side. Cover with a generous layer of tomato suace.
Next pour on the Tofu mixture, spreading evenly, being
careful not to mix with the sauce. Repeat with a layer of
noodles, remaining sauce, ending with the cheese. Bake
at 350° for 30 min.

Italics indicate item in index

SPAGHETTI

Whole grain spaghetti, cooked. *Pizza* Sauce, hot.
Cashew Pimento Cheese Sauce. *Italian Meatballs*, cooked.
Serve along with a tossed salad, bread and *Sun Seed
Spread*.

COOKING CHART FOR BEANS

Beans (Soaked)	Amount of Water to Cover Top of Beans (in ")	Cooking Tim
Lentils, Split Peas, Mung Beans	1"	45-60 min.
Black,Kidney, Baby Lima, Pinto, Navy Beans	2"	2-2½ hrs.
Garbanzo (Chick Peas), Soybeans	3"	3½ - 4½ hrs

Wash beans in a colander under running water. Check for
pebbles. Cover beans with about 3 times more water than
beans. Let them soak at least 6 hours. The main purpose
for soaking is to shorten cooking time. This saves an
hour or more depending on the bean used. Lentils, split
peas and mung beans will not cook faster if soaked
therefore skip this step. Salt in beans delays cooking.
When beans are tender add 1 t. of salt per quart of
cooked beans. Next is a very important point. Bring
the beans and water to a boil, in a covered sauce pan,
then turn the heat down to low or med. low for a light
boil. Check occasionally in case more water is needed.
If using a crockpot over night be sure it comes up to a
simmer. 1 c. dry beans = 2½ - 2 3/4 c. cooked.

SOY GARBANZO SOUFFLE

1½ c. *soaked soy, garbanzo*   1/2 c. onion, chopped
  (or mixed) *beans*   1 garlic clove
2 c. tomato juice or stewed   1/2 t. basil
  tomatoes   1/3 t. salt
1/4 c. olives, chopped

Blend smooth all but olives and onion. Stir all ingredients and pour into an oiled 8 x 8 baking dish. Bake,
uncovered, at 350° for 60 min. Serve hot or cold, plain
or with *Ketchup*, as a sandwich filling or main dish.

Italics indicate item in index

EASY BEANS
4 c. cooked, dried peas or beans, unsalted
4 t. *Yeast Paste*
1/2 c. onion, chopped, cooked
1/4 t. garlic powder

Combine all together, heat and serve.

HAYSTACKS
Cashew Pimento Cheese Sauce or *Golden Sauce*
Easy Beans, hot
Fritos, Dodgers, Croutons or corn chips

Place the crackers on a plate. Spoon on beans. Layer with your choice of the following: chopped tomatoes, shredded lettuce, diced onions, alfalfa *Sprouts*. Top with sauce.

BLACK BEANS AND RICE
1½ c. black beans, dried	1 bay leaf
3½ c. water	1¼ t. salt
1/2 c. onions, chopped	1½ t. onion powder
1/2 c. green pepper, chopped	2 T. lemon juice
1 lg. clove garlic, minced	

Soak beans in water and follow directions from *Cooking Chart for Beans*. (Cook beans in same water as used for soaking.) When beans are almost tender add remaining ingredients and continue cooking until beans are soft. Serve over brown rice. Another way to prepare is to simmer in a crockpot several hours. Yield 4½ c.

BAKED BEANS
6 c. cooked pinto or navy beans, unsalted	1 onion, chopped
1 c. water or bean water	2 garlic cloves, minced
1-16 oz. can of tomatoes chopped, optional	1/4 c. molasses
	2 t. salt

Mix all ingredients together. Cook in a sauce pan until onion is tender. Or bake, uncovered, at 350° for 60 min.

Italics indicate item in index

CHICKPEA A LA KING

3 c. water, for beans
1 c. garbanzo beans, dried
1/2 c. onions, chopped
1/2 c. *nuts or seeds*
1/4 c. flour

3 T. *chicken style seasoni*
1 t. salt
3 c. additional water or
  garbanzo cooking water
1½ c. green peas, frozen
1/4 c. pimento, chopped, o

To prepare beans follow instructions on *Cooking Chart for Beans* using the 3 c. of water in recipe for soaking and cooking beans. After beans are done drain them. Use this water as part of the additional water recipe calls for. *Blend* smooth: 3/4 c. leftover water, nuts, flour, chicken seasoning and salt. Then add remaining 2¼ c. of liquid. Pour into saucepan. Bring to a boil, stirring frequently. Let simmer 5 min then add remaining ingredients. Bring back up to a boil, then simmer about 10-15 min or until vegetables are tender, stirring occassionally. Serve over brown rice. Yield 1½ qt.

SCRAMBLED "EGG" TOFU

1/2 c. onions, chopped
1 lb. *Tofu*, mashed
2 t. dried chives
2 t. *chicken style seasoning*

1/4 - 1/2 t. salt
1/2 t. onion powder
1/8 t. garlic powder

Saute onions in small amount of water. Add remaining ingredients, heat and serve. Serve hot or cold. Plain or with *Ketchup*. As a main dish or sandwich filling.

BAKED TOFU

1 lb *Tofu*

Cut tofu in 1/4" thick slices. Lightly sprinkle salt on both sides. Bake in a toaster oven or put cake racks on regular grates in an oven. Lay slices directly on racks. Bake at 350° for 40 min. Chewy outside, tender inside. Eat plain or with a spread. With a fruit or vegetable meal.

Italics indicate item in index

TOFU OATBURGER LOAF
1 recipe *Oatburger*   1 lb of *Tofu*, mashed

Follow the directions for preparing the oatburger.
Instead of making patties combine with tofu and bake in
an oiled 1½ qt. casserole at 350° for 45 min. Serve with
gravy.

TOFU PATTIES
1 lb *Tofu*	2 T. *Yeast Flakes*
3½ c. quick or rolled oats	2 t. salt
1 c. water	1/2 t. marjoram
1 med. onion, quartered	1/4 t. thyme
2 garlic clove	

Blend all ingredients smooth except oats. Stir oats in.
Form into patties and bake at 350° for 30 min on an oiled
cookie sheet. Turn over and bake an additional 10 min

Makes 12. Serve with gravy, *Cheese Sauce,Ketchup.*

TOFU QUICHE-BASIC RECIPE
1/2 lb *Tofu*	1/4 t. salt
2/3 c. water	2 T. flour
1/2 c. *Cashew Pimento Cheese*	
Sauce	

Blend smooth all ingredients. Pour into an 8" baked pie
crust. (Increase this recipe by half if not using any
of the variations.) Or pour into a small casserole dish
with no crust. Bake at 350° for 30 min, until center is
firm. Let sit 5 min before serving. If dish is not
being sliced to serve cooking time and fuel may be
saved by cooking ingredients in a sauce pan, stirring,
about 10 min, or until it thickens. Pour into a serving
dish and let set a few min before serving.

Variations:
Vegetable Quiche
   add to the basic recipe:

1/2 c. onion, chopped	1/2 t. basil
1½ c. broccoli, chopped	1/2 t. salt
or 1-10 oz. frozen package	

Italics indicate item in index

Cook vegetables in a small amount of water, drain. Add,
with the seasonings, to the basic recipe. Bake as directe
Other vegetables may substitute broccoli, i.e., greens,
carrots and potatoes, green beans and celery, all onions
with a clove of garlic etc.

Italian Quiche
   add to the basic recipe:

1/2 c. tomato paste   3/4 t. basil
1/4 c. water   1/2 t. salt
1 T. cornstarch   1/4 t. garlic powder
1/2 c. onion, chopped   1/4 t. oregano
1/4 c. green pepper, chopped
2 t. lemon juice

Cook onion and pepper in small amount of water. Stir all
ingredients together and add to the basic recipe. Bake
as directed.

SCALLOPED POTATOES

4 c. water   2 t. Italian Seasoning
1 c. peanuts, raw or dry   5 c. potatoes, thinnly sliced
   roasted   1½ c. onions, thinnly sliced
1½ t. salt

Blend smooth 1 c. of the water with nuts and seasonings.
Add remining water. Layer potatoes and onions in a
large casserole. Fill it no more than half full. Pour
sauce over. Cover. Bake at 350° for 30 min. Uncover
and continue to bake 20-30 min. Serve as is or top with
Cashew Pimento Cheese Sauce during last 10 min of baking.

VEGETABLE POT PIE

1 c. green peas   1 c. *Peanut Meat*, chopped,
1/2 c. onions, chopped   optional
1 c. carrots, diced   2½ c. gravy or 1 recipe of
1 c. white potatoes, diced   *Potato Gravey*
                                Whole Wheat Pie Crust

Cook vegetables until tender. Stir in peanut meat and
gravy. Any of the gravy recipes given in the cookbook
would be fine. If desiring a bottom crust use a double

Italics Indicate item in index

recipe for the crust and lightly oil a 1½ qt. casserole.
Cover bottom and sides with portion of crust. Fill with
vegetable mixture and top with remaining crust. Poke
a few holes in the crust then bake at 350° for 45-50 min.

Variations:
Use any cooked, dried bean or pea for green peas. Use
other vegetables in season. Try rolling out 1/4" thick
Whole Wheat Bread dough as the crust. Bake as mentioned
above.

HARDY HASH

2 c. rice, cooked	2 c. potatoes, raw, shredded
1/2 c. onions, chopped	1/2 t. salt
1/2 c. chopped *nuts or seeds*	1 clove garlic, minced
1/4 c. *yeast flakes*	2 t. *Yeast Paste*

Mix all ingredients. Simmer gently in non stick or
lightly oiled skillet, uncovered, not stirring, 10 min.
Scrape from bottom and turn. Cover and cook additional
20 min or until done.

STUFFED PEPPERS OR ZUCCHINI

Wash medium size peppers, cut off tops, remove seeds and
parboil in salted water 3-5 min, drain. Or wash medium
size, 8" zucchini, cut off stem tip, cut in half length-
wise. Scoop out center, leaving a thin shell. Parboil
the same as the peppers.

Stuff with one of the following unbaked mixes from the
entree section (portion removed from zucchini may be added
to the stuffing):

*Italian Meatballs, Millet Patties, Pecan Loaf, Spanish
Rice, Lentil Loaf.*

Top with 1-2 T.of *Cashew Pimento Cheese Sauce, Agar
Cheese* or *Golden Sauce.* Bake, covered, at 350° for
35 min.

Italics indicate item in index

MISCELLANEOUS

SOY BASE

2 c. water   1 t. salt
1 c. soy flour

Blend or stir all until smooth. After cooking, base
should be custard consistency. Methods of cooking:
1. In oven in an uncovered dish at 350° for 35 min.
    (stir after 20 min.)
2. On top of stove using a simmer ring under a covered
    sauce pan. Cook on medium low heat, stirring
    occasionally for 30 min.
3. In a double boiler, covered, stirring occasionally.
    Cook for 2 hrs.
4. In covered crockpot on medium (use low if pot has
    no medium) for about 3-4 hrs. Stir occasionally.
Soy base will keep in refrigerator 2 weeks or may be
frozen. Freezing in ½ c. proportions in plastic bags
is convenient for many recipes.

YEAST PASTE

This product may be used in place of the commercial
pastes such as *Vegex*, *SoVex* and *Savorex*. In this recipe
the soy sauce is replaced by toasted sesame seeds.
1/2 c. sesame seeds, toasted   1/3 c. *coffee substitute,*
1 3/4 c. *yeast flakes*   i.e. Postum
3 T. salt   1/2 c. water
                               1/4 c. lemon juice

Toast seeds in a dry skillet on medium heat, stirring
frequently, until golden brown. *Blend* smooth seeds
and water. Pour into mixing bowl and stir all ingredients together. Keep refrigerated. Use in same proportions as if using commercial yeast paste. Will keep
several weeks in refrigerator. May freeze if desire.

SOY SAUCE

1/4 c. water   3 T. *Yeast Paste*

Dissolve paste into water. Refrigerate. Use in same
way as commercial soy sauce.

Italics indicate item in index

CHICKEN STYLE SEASONING
1 1/3 c. *yeast flakes*
3 T. onion powder
2½ t. garlic powder
2½ T. salt

1 t. celery seed
2½ T. Italian Seasoning
2 T. parsley, dried

Blend smooth all except parsley. Stir parsley in. Seal
in an airtight container. May use in same proportion as
when using McKays Chicken Style Seasoning.

SESAME SALT
1 c. sesame seeds   1 t. salt

Roast seeds over medium heat in a dry skillet until
lightly browned. Add salt and *blend* leaving some seeds
partially whole. Sprinkle over salads, vegetables,
rice. Add to entrees or burgers before cooking.

CUCUMBER RELISH
3 qt. shredded cucumbers
3 lg. onions, chopped
1/2 c. salt
1 c. lemon juice

1 c. cucumber juice
1 c. *sweetener*
1 t. celery seed
3 bay leaves

Allow shredded cucumbers to drain about 4 hrs. Combine
all ingredients except cucumbers and onions. Bring
to a boil then simmer 3 min. Add cucs and onions. Boil,
lightly for 10 min. Pour into hot, sterilized jars and
seal.

PICKLES
2 t. salt
2 t. dill seed
1/4 c. lemon juice

2 garlic cloves
3/4 c. water

Boil water, salt and juice 3 min. Place cucumber
wedges or slices in a quart jar. Add remaining ingredients.
If necessary add more hot water. Leave 1" head space.
Boil in hot water bath for 10 min.

Italics indicate item in index

65

CANNED WHOLE GRAINS

1¼ c. whole grain   3/4 t. salt

Place grain and salt in a quart jar. Fill to shoulder
of jar with water. Process at 10# for 1 hour. Try
using *berries*, rice, hulled barley or millet. Convenient
for trips or camping. Heat and serve.

CANNED BEANS

1 1/2 c. dried beans or peas
1 t. salt

Place washed, sorted legumes in a quart jar. Add water
to the shoulder of the jar. Process for 1½ hour at
10 pounds pressure.

NIGHTSHADE REPLACEMENTS

Many arthritics are sensitive to the nightshade family
(tomato, white potato, hot and sweet peppers, eggplant
and tobacco). For them these recipes are added.

UN-TOMATO KETCHUP

1 c. carrots, cooked   1/2 t. salt
1/4 c. beets, cooked   1/2 t. onion powder
1/4 c. water   1/4 t. garlic powder
1/4 c. lemon juice   1/8 t. oregano
1 T. *sweetener*

Blend until smooth.

UN-FRENCH DRESSING

1/3 c. carrot, cooked   1½ t. onion powder
1½ T. beet, cooked   1/2 t. garlic powder
2/3 c. water   1 t. *sweetener*
1/4 c. lemon juice   1/2 t. salt
1/3 c. *nuts or seeds*
Blend smooth all ingredients

Italics indicate item in index

66

CARROT CHEESE SAUCE
Follow recipe for *Cashew Pimento Cheese Sauce* . Omit
pimento and use 2/3 c. cooked carrots. Add a small amount
of additional water, if necessary, to blend. May use
any of the variations listed as well. Use in making
Macaroni and Cheese (see Entree Section for directions).

CARROT CHEESE SPREAD
Follow the recipe for *Cashew Cheese Spread.* Omit the
pimento replacing it with 1/3 c. cooked carrots. Reduce
oats to 1/4 c. Any *nut or seed* may replace cashews.

CARROT NUT CHEESE
Follow recipe for *Nut Cheese.* Replace tomatoes with 1/3
c. cooked carrots. Use the amount of salt called for
or replace it with 1 T. *Yeast Paste.*

UN-TOMATO SOUP

2 c. *Soy Milk*	1/4 t. basil
1 c. water	1/4 t. garlic powder
1 c. carrots, cooked	1½ t. onion powder
3 T. beets, cooked	3/4 t. salt
2 T. cornstarch	1 t. *sweetener*
4 t. lemon juice	1/16 t. oregano

Blend smooth all but soy milk. Pour milk and blended
portion into a sauce pan. Cook about 10-15 min, stirring,
until slightly thickened.

UN-TOMATO CHILI

2 c. carrots, cooked	1 c. onions, chopped, cooked
1/2 c. beets, cooked	3 T. lemon juice
3¼ c. water or bean broth	1 garlic clove
6½ c. cooked Kidney or	1 t. basil
Pinto beans, unsalted	1/2 t. oregano
1 T. salt	1½ T. *sweetener*

Blend smooth all but beans and onion. Combine all
ingredients, heat and serve.

Italics indicate item in index

67

UN-TOMATO PIZZA

2½ c. carrots, cooked
1/2 c. beets, cooked
2/3 c. water
2 T. lemon juice
3/4 t. salt

1/2 t. basil
1/2 t. onion powder
1/8 t. oregano
1/2 c. onions, chopped,
    cooked
1 garlic clove, minced

Blend all ingredients except the onion and garlic.
Cooked onion and garlic in a small amount of water.
Stir all ingredients together. See *Pizza* in the Entree
Section for remaining instructions concerning the crust
and assembly of pizza. Top with *Carrot Cheese Sauce*.

Un-TOMATO LASAGNA

Carrot Cheese Sauce, *Un-Tomato Pizza* sauce, hot,
double recipe. Follow the instructions and remaining
needed items from *Lasagna* in the Entree Section. Omit
the pizza and cheese sauce listed there and instead
use what is listed above.

UN-TOMATO SPAGHETTI

Whole grain spaghetti, cooked. *Un-Tomato Pizza* sauce,
hot. *Carrot Cheese Sauce*. *Italian Meatballs*, cooked.
Serve along with tossed salad,
bread and spread.

CAULIFLOWER "POTATO" SALAD

See recipe for *Potato Salad*. Replace potatoes with
cooked, chopped cauliflower.

SALADS

SPROUTS

In all food preparation, it is desirable to make
individual dishes simple, and to serve few dishes at
a meal. Care should be used that salads are not complex
mixtures. If part of the cooked food for the meal is
made from carrots, cabbage, celery, greens or tomato,
use these same items as a part of the salad.

Italics Indicate item in index

Use one to three vegetables together depending on how many varieties are being cooked, and serve this attractively. Be artistic using a variety of methods for preparation such as slicing, dicing, shredding.

Sprouts are very economical and highly nutritious. They may be used several times a week. Sprouting seeds, beans and grains: Almost any whole natural seed can be sprouted. Be sure to buy untreated seeds. They can be obtained in health food departments.

1. Put seeds, grain or beans in quart jar. Cover with water 3 times the amount of seed. Soak 8-12 hours.

2. Secure a piece of fiberglass mesh, hardware cloth or other permeable material (not aluminum treated window screen) over the top of the jar. Use a jar ring or cut the middle out of a lid and screw on over the screen. Cheese cloth or nylon stocking material will work but are not as easy to handle during the rinsing stage. Sprouting tops can be purchased in health food stores.

3. Pour off water. Add more to rinse seeds then drain. Invert jar for several min in a dish drainer or bowl to thoroughly drain. Rinse twice daily. Some beans spoil rather easily and should be rinsed 3 or 5 times daily in hot humid weather. Never leave sprouts sitting in water.

4. After bean or grain sprouts have reached desired length rinse one final time. Drain well on a paper towel then refrigerate in plastic bag. With alfalfa,radish and other small seeds place them in a bowl. Cover with water and gently swish in a circular motion. Most of the brown hulls will float to the rim or sink to the bottom. Scoop out the ones on top. Don't try to get them all! Drain well on towel then spread on a cookie sheet. Cover with plastic wrap. Make a few slits in wrap for air. Place sprouts in sunlight for 4-6 hrs. This will develop the chlorophyll (green color) which gives added nutrition.

5. Cooking – seeds and grains, sprouted may be eaten raw. Beans and peas will be more digestible, therefore more nutritious, if allowed to steam 15–20 min.

Grains, beans and peas are generally best when sprouts are 1/2 – 3/4" long. Many beans may grow 1 -1½". Alfalfa, radish and other small seeds may also grow 1 - 1½" and be tasty. Use 1 T. of alfalfa for 1 qt. of sprouts. 2 T of radish, cabbage and red clover; 1/4 c. mung beans, 1/2 c. unhulled grains, i.e., *berries*; 1 c. of peas and beans to produce about 1 quart of sprouts. Most sprouts take 4-5 days to reach desired length.

POTATO SALAD

2 c. cooked potatoes, cubed
1 c. celery, finely diced
1/4 c. onion, diced
1/4 c. olives, slices

2 T. fresh parsley, chopped
2 T. lemon juice
3/4 c. *soy garbanzo* or
   soy mayonnaise

Mix all together. Chill several hours.

THREE BEAN SALAD

1½ c. cooked kidney beans, salted (or 15 oz. can)
1½ c. cooked garbanzo beans, salted (or 15 oz. can)
1 3/4 c. green or wax beans, salted (or 15½ oz. can)
1/4 c. onions, minced, or 1/2 c. celery, diced
1/4 c. olives, sliced, optional
2 T. pimento, diced optional

1/4 c. lemon juice
1/4 c. water
3 T. *sweetener*

1/2 t. onion powder
1/4 t. garlic powder
3/4 t. salt

Stir vegetables and olives together. Combine lemon juice, water and seasonings together. Mix all together well. Chill. Yield. 5 cups. Marinate several hours before serving.

Italics indicate item in index

S O U P S

FRUIT SOUP
1/2 c. tapioca
1/2 c. dried apricot pieces
4 c. pineapple juice
4 c. orange juice

2 c. apples, diced
1 c. pineapple chunks
2 oranges, chopped

Place tapioca and pineapple juice in a sauce pan. Let
sit 5 min. Bring to a boil, stirring, reduce heat to a
simmer and cook until tapioca is clear. Add remaining
ingredients. Chill. Substitute any fruit in season.
Keep it simple, 3 or 4 fruits.

CHILI
4 c. soaked kidney beans
3/4 c. onions, chopped
1 c. green peppers chopped
3/4 t. basil
1 t. onion powder

3/4 quart tomatoes
1 clove garlic, minced
1 T. *sweetener*
1½ t. salt

Soak beans overnight in water twice their volume. Pour
off water and cover with fresh water about 2" above
beans. Simmer 1½ hrs. Add remaining ingredients to
beans. Cook 45-60 min. Serve with *cornbread muffins,
better butter,* salad and dressing.

LIMA BEAN CHOWDER
1 c. onions, chopped
2 c. potatoes, diced
1/2 c. whole kernel corn
1 c. lima beans, either
   fresh, frozen or cooked
   dried beans

4 c. *soy milk*
3 T. flour
1 1/2 t. salt
1 clove garlic, minced

Cook vegetables until tender. Stir flour into milk,
simmer, stirring, 10-15 min. Add remaining ingredients,
reheat and serve.

Italics indicate item in index

CREAM OF TOMATO SOUP

2 c. *Soy Milk*
1½ t. onion powder
3/4 t. salt
1/8 t. oregano
1½ t. *sweetener*

1/3 c. flour
1/4 t. garlic powder
1 qt. tomatoes
1/4 t. basil

Blend tomatoes and dry ingredients until smooth. Mix all ingredients. Cook 15-20 min, stirring often.

SPLIT PEA CHOWDER

6 c. water
1/2 c. brown rice
2 c. split peas
2 t. salt

1 c. onions, chopped
1/2 c. carrots, diced
1/2 c. celery, diced
1/2 t. basil

Add rice and peas to boiling water, cook 1½ hrs. Add remaining ingredients and continue to cook about 30 min. Vegetables will be crisp.

GARBANZO CHICKEN NOODLE SOUP

4½ c. water
1 c. *soaked garbanzo beans*
1/2 c. uncooked whole grain
   noodles
1 med. onion, chopped

1 bay leaf
2 t. *Chicken Style*
  Seasoning
1 t. parsley, dried
1/4 c.*Tofu* diced, optional

Cook beans in water until soft. Add remaining ingredient and simmer 25 min.

VEGETABLES

There are many different ways to make vegetables taste well seasoned without over using salt or oil, and still avoiding harmful substances such as vinegar, pepper and other undesirable spices.

Several of the dressings, (i.e. *Hummus, Savory Bouquet, Soy Garbanzo Mayonnaise)* spreads (i.e. *Sun Seed Spread,*

Italics indicate item in index

72

Better Butter, Millet Butter, Fresh Corn Butter, Cheese Spread) or the *Cashew Pimento Cheese Sauce* make vegetables new and interesting. *Golden Sauce* over broccoli or carrots is delicious. Lemon or lime juice, tomato sauce, onion or garlic (fresh or powder), sweet peppers, chives or parsley might be just the thing to give added zest to nicely cooked vegetables. When using herbs to enhance flavor experiment, beginning with small amounts. Long cooking destroys their flavor. If cooking time is more than an hour add herbs during last hour. If using fresh herbs use 3 times more than if normally using dried.

Steaming in a pan with a tight fitting lid helps preserve nutrients. Whether boiling or steaming save leftover cooking water. This water may contain 50% or more of the water soluble nutrients from the food. Use the water to cook more vegetables, dried beans or whole grains, or to make gravy, soup, patties, a loaf, dressing, bread, waffles or crackers.

SAUTEING VEGETABLES WITHOUT FAT OR OIL
Place a little water in skillet. Add chopped vegetables and cook on low or medium heat until tender. Stir as needed. A little extra water may be needed while cooking.

GREEN BEANS IN CASSEROLE
Place cooked beans in casserole. Pour gravy over beans and top with bread crumbs. Bake at 350° for 20-30 min.

GLAZED BEETS WITH LEMON SAUCE
4 c. beets, cooked, sliced	1/4 t. salt
1 c. beet juice or water	2 T. lemon juice
2 T. starch	1 T. *sweetener*

Cook juice, starch and salt together, stirring, until clear and thick. Remove from heat, add remaining ingredients. More salt will be needed if beets are saltfree.

Italics indicate item in index

DILLY GREEN BEANS

2 c. green beans, cooked
1/2 c. onion, chopped
1 garlic clove, minced

1/2 t. dill seed or weed
Salt to taste
1/4 c. water

Cook onion, garlic and dill in water or bean juice.
When tender add beans. Heat and serve.

SWEET AND SOUR CABBAGE

1 med head red cabbage (2#), shredded
1/4 c. onion, chopped
1/3 c. *sweetener*
1/3 c. lemon juice

1 t. caraway seed
1 t. salt

Mix all but cabbage. Stir all together in saucepan.
Cover and simmer until cabbage is tender. About 15 min.

STEAMED CABBAGE

4 c. cabbage, chopped
1/4 c. water, boiling

2 t. *Chicken Style
    Seasoning*
1/2 t. caraway seed, option

Add ingredients to boiling water. Cover. Steam 10
min, until tender.

Variations:
1. Replace half of cabbage with shredded carrots.
2. Substitute shredded turnips or rutabaga for cabbage.
   Steam a few min longer. May need to add more
   water. Stir occasionally.

CORN SESAME COMBO

2 c. fresh or frozen corn
1 clove garlic, minces
2 T. sesame seed, toasted

2 T. green pepper, chopped
1/2 t. salt
1/4 t. basil leaves

Place sesame seeds in dry fry pan. Stir over med heat
a few min. Cook all ingredients together until tender.

Italics indicate item in index

EGGPLANT OR ZUCCHINI STACKS

Large zucchini or peeled
  eggplant
Tomato Slices
Onion slices

Green pepper slices
Cashew Pimento Cheese Sauce
or Agar Cheese

Slice zucchini or eggplant in 3/8" slices, allowing 2-4
good-sized slices per person. If using eggplant, soak
slices in salted water 1/4 hr. (1½ t. salt per 1 qt
water). This step is optional but it seems to help
eliminate the slightly harsh or bitter taste that is
characteristic of eggplant. Drain slices and place on
oiled cookie sheet, sprinkle with salt if did not soak
in salt water. Place a slice of tomato on each eggplant
or zucchini, sprinkle a few grains of salt, add a
slice of onion and green pepper followed with a few
grains of salt. Bake at 400° for 45 min. Top each
stack with as much cheese as desired. Cheese will be
thicker and more will stay on each stack if it is
chilled before using. Bake additional 20 min.

FRENCH FRIES

Boil potatoes 20 min. Peel (opt.) Cut as fries.
Place on cookie sheet, oiled, one layer thick. Lightly
sprinkle with salt. Bake 400° for 45-60 min. Turn
after 25 min with a spatula.

SWEET POTATO SOUFFLE

3 c. sweet potatoes, cooked
1 c. almond milk or *soy milk*

1/4 t. salt
2 T. coconut

See recipe for *Nut Milk* using almonds for the nuts to
be used. Mash, skinned sweet potatoes, with a fork or
potato masher. Mix with milk and salt. Place in oiled
casserole. Top with coconut. Bake, uncovered, at
350° for 45 min.

Italics indicate item in index

ZUCCHINI, CORN AND TOMATOES

2 med. size zucchini, about 2# or 4 c. sliced
1/2 c. onion, thinly sliced
1 3/4 t. salt
1/2 t. oregano
3/4 t. basil
2½ c. tomatoes, fresh or canned, chopped
1½ c. corn
1/4 c. water

Slice thinly zucchini on diagonal. Combine all ingredients, bring to a boil then simmer gently to desired tenderness. Serve as is or over brown rice or noodles. Top with *Cashew Pimento Cheese Sauce.*

Italics indicate item in index

DIET AND DISEASE*

Diverticular disease, ischemic heart disease, gall stones, appendicitis, varicose veins, hiatus hernia, and cancer are all common problems in the United States. And yet among rural Africans and in other places where contact with the western world and its diet has only been recent these diseases can be described as being very rare. Ischemic heart disease is almost non-existent. Diverticular disease has a prevalence of substantially less than one percent.

In reply to a questionnaire sent to rural hospitals in Africa, ten doctors, each with more than 20 years experience there, reported they had never seen one African with gallstones. Monthly returns were received from 84 hospitals in 13 countries in Africa during a two year period. Only 15 recorded even a single patient with gallstones and none reported more than two patients a year. One doctor with 33 years experience in a mission hospital, in a less developed part of Africa, is still awaiting his first case of appendicitis. In correspondence with the medical journal, Lancet, a doctor with 22 years experience in Africa wrote that he had seen only three cases of varicose veins. More than 70,000 new cases of cancer of the colon and rectum are diagnosed in the United States annually. Yet, in African communities living in a traditional way, bowel cancer is rare.

In an article entitled "When the Eskimo comes to town" we read of the plight of Canadian eskimoes who became "cultured" almost overnight. In 1959 the average Eskimo was consuming only 26 lbs of sugar a year. By 1967 the figure had shot up to 104 lbs. Some of the results reported are the emergence of diabetes, a marked increase in gallbladder disease and atherosclerosis, not to mention acne and dental caries. Prior to 1950 no operations for gallbladder disease had ever been reported among the eskimoes but now they outnumber all other operations.

Careful studies have shown an increase in many diseases among Japanese after they move from Japan to California or Hawaii and adopt the western diet. In light of these examples one can readily see the wisdom of our heavenly Father in providing whole fruits, nuts, grains, and vegetables for our food. How much better it would be if all would eat their food as God provided it for them. (Genesis 2:20, 3:18)

*Based on articles,
"Economic Development not All Bonus," Dennis Burkitt, M.D., <u>Nutrition Today</u>. Jan, Feb. 1976.

"When the Eskimo Comes to Town." Otto Schaefer, M.D. <u>Nutrition Today</u>. Nov/Dec. 1971.

INSTRUCTIONS ON EATING

The disease and suffering that everywhere prevail are largely due to popular errors in regard to diet. What we eat and drink today, walks and talks tomorrow. By carefully heeding the following instructions you may avoid many illnesses:

1. Eat largely of fruits, grains, and vegetables prepared in a natural yet tasty way. Limit rich foods, keeping sugars to 3 teaspoons, salt to 7/8 teaspoon, and oil to 2 tablespoons daily. Fruit juices and other concentrated foods usually should be taken in small quantities.

2. Vary your diet from meal to meal but do not eat too many varieties at any one meal. A main dish, along with an additional cooked and raw dish plus bread with a spread and/or dressing is a plan which may be helpful.

3. Use more of the whole grains and less food prepared from refined grains. Cooked cereals are generally better than dry cereals unless using a cereal made with little or no honey, sugar or oil.

4. Eat at the same mealtime daily and allow at least 5 hours from the end of one meal to the beginning of the next. This includes any item with caloric value such as juice, mints, chewing gum, fruits, etc., as they will delay the digestion of food already in the stomach from the previous meal.

5. Eat a substantial breakfast which should more nearly correspond to the largest meal of the day. Eat only a light supper, fruit and whole grains, (such as an apple and a few crackers without butter), and this two or three hours or more before retiring so that the stomach may also rest.

6. Eat all you need to maintain health, and enjoy your food, but don't overeat. Too much food dulls and depresses the mind, causing disease and fatigue and shortens life.

7. Eating slowly and chewing your food thoroughly will increase the enjoyment as well as the nutritional benefits derived from it.

8. Drink enough water daily to keep the urine quite pale, but do not drink with your meals or immediately before or after them as this will delay digestion.

9. The following are a list of what are dangerous foods. Total abstinence is recommended: spices such as hot pepper (black or red), ginger, cinnamon, cloves, nutmeg, cumin, mustard and horseradish. These are items which in their cold state are hot to the tongue. Also baking powder and soda, vingar, spoiled, aged or fermented foods including ketchup, mayonnaise, ripened (or hard cheese). Also pressed or ground meats, rare,

treated or aged meats. All of these will irritate
the gastrointestinal tract, particularly the stomach,
can cause fermentation, noticeable by gas and will
create a burden on the digestive system. Combina-
tions of large quantities of milk and sugar, with or
without eggs, such as in custards, ice cream,
sherberts and cakes or combining fruits and vegetables
in the same meal lead to fermentation in the stomach
and eventually weakening the system. Coffee, tea,
chocolate and some soft drinks contain caffeine or
similar substances which have many harmful effects
including: aids in the production of ulcers, raises
the blood pressure, increases the heart rate,
aggrevates hypoglycemia and diabetes, contributes
to coronary heart disease, increases risk of stomach
and bladder cancer, crosses the placenta and affects
the unborn child and is an addictive drug.

EATING BETWEEN MEALS

X-ray studies conducted to determine the emptying time
of the normal stomach shows the average to be between
four and five hours. A study was run using several
persons who were given a routine breakfast consisting
of cereal and cream, bread, cooked fruit and an egg.
Their stomachs were x-rayed and found to be empty in
four and one-half hours.

A few days later these same persons were given the same
type of breakfast and two hours later they were fed
snacks, their emptying time was checked. The results
are shown on the next page.

80

NORMAL BREAKFAST	TWO HOURS LATER	RESULTS
Person No. 1	Ice cream cone	Residue in the stomach after 6 hours
Person No. 2	Peanut butter sandwich	Residue after 9 hours
Person No. 3	Pumpkin pie, glass of milk	Residue after 9 hours
Person No. 4	Half slice of bread and butter repeated every one and one-half hour interval and no dinner	More than half his breakfast in stomach after 9 hours
Person No. 5	Twice in the morning and twice in the afternoon a bit of chocolate candy	Thirteen and one-half hours later more than one-half the morning meal was still in the stomach

81

FIBER

Fiber can be defined as that portion of food which is not digested or absorbed. It is the plant residue which reaches the colon.

Dr. Dennis Burkitt was the keynote lecturer at the second annual Bristol-Meyers-Symposium on Nutrition Research. There he spoke of the strongly implicated relationship between a lack of fiber in the diet and many diseases including, diverticular disease, gall stones and cancer of the colon. Meat, refined cereals, sugar, visible fats (oils), milk and eggs are all non-fiber foods. Whole grains, beans, nuts, fruits and vegetables are good sources of fiber. Americans are now getting only about 10% of their calories from these sources. The length of time it takes the average American intestinal tract to process a meal is over 70 hours as compared to less than 30 hours for African villagers. This is directly related to fiber intake. The slow transit time is a fruitful cause of disease.

SUGAR AND THE BODY

The average American consumes 35 teaspoons of sugar each day. Most people are unaware of the amounts of sugar in ordinary pastries, desserts, drinks, and snack foods. Listed below are a few common foods and the actual amounts of sugar hidden in them.

An important fact about sugar has to do with disease resistance. Our white blood cells destroy bacteria. However, when the blood sugar level goes up these cells get sluggish. Think of the significance of the following chart when each white blood cell is multiplied by the 60 to 400 trillion phagocytic white blood cells active in the human body.

EFFECT OF SUGAR INTAKE ON ABILITY OF WHITE BLOOD CELLS TO DESTROY BACTERIA

Teaspoons of sugar eaten at one time by average adult.	Number of bacteria destroyed by each WBC in 30 minutes.	Percentage decrease in ability to destroy bacteria.
0	14	0
6	10	25
12	5.5	60
18	2	85
24	1	92
Uncontrolled diabetic	1	92

HIDDEN SUGAR

	Teaspoons sugar		
Chocolate bar, average size	7	Apple pie, 1/6 pie	7
Chocolate fudge, 1½ square	4	Pumpkin pie, 1/6 pie	5
Marshmallow, 1 average	1.5	Chocolate milk, 1 cup	6
Chewing gum, 1 stick	0.5	Cocoa, 1 cup	4
Chocolate cake, 1½" piece	12	Banana split	20
Doughnut, glazed	8	Jam, 1 T.	3
Brownie, 2" x 2" x 3/4"	3	Honey, 1 T	3
Ice Cream, 1/2 cup	5-6	Jelly, 1 T	2½
Sherbert, 1/2 cup	6-8	Peaches, canned, 2 halves	3½

83

P R O T E I N *

The recommended daily allowance for protein in the
United States is 56 grams for men and 46 grams for
women. The World Health Organization recommends 37
grams daily for men and 29 for women. The United
States Senate committee on nutrition recommends that
approximately 12% of our caloric intake be in the form
of protein. They recognized however in their <u>Dietary
Goals for the United States</u> that "..... the average
American eats daily almost twice as much protein ..."
as is recommended.

With greens and legumes averaging approximately 23%
of their calories as protein and fruits and grains
approximately 8% it is easy to see that the complete
vegetarian gets the recommended 12% with no problem.
The United States R.D.A.s have a 30 to 50% safety
margin added to them. This is seen in the fact that
the daily calorie recommendation is 2700 calories which
amount few people need. If, however the complete
vegetarian averaging about 12% of his calories as
protein would eat the 2700 calories he would be getting
81 grams of protein daily. Even if he were to dilute
his calories with sugar and refined foods by as much
as 50% he would still be getting the minimum daily
requirement.

Science indicates that the 100-plus grams a day protein
intake of the average non-vegetarian American puts
a tax on the liver and kidneys, triggers a loss of
calcium from the bones, and also leaves behind a toxic
residue which before being eliminated often damages
the body and thus makes it more susceptable to a
variety of diseases, including cancer and arthritis.

The loss of calcium from the bones of course leads
to osteoporosis which is much more common among meat
eaters than vegetarians. The latter group needs less
calcium. Quoting Alfred E. Harper, Ph. D., Chairman
of the Committee on Recommended Dietary Allowances

of the Food and Nutrition Board, National Academy of
Sciences - National Research Council:

> The calcium allowance was discussed at length
> by the committeee .... Information derived from
> recent studies indicates that, for adults with
> a protein intake as low as the current RDA (56 gm
> men, 46 gm women), about 500 mg or calcium per day
> should be adequate, (other nutritionists believe
> even 350 mg would be adequate), and this is recog-
> nized in the text. <u>Nevertheless</u>, the allowance
> (recommended) was left at 800 mg per day. (the
> 1968 level) because of the high protein intakes
> prevalent in the U.S. ... This leaves the allowances
> for calcium <u>well above</u> those of Canada, the
> United Kingdom, and FAO/WHO.

Nutrition Today, March-April, 1974, pages 20, 21.

* For a more complete discussion with references,
you may order from Family Health Publications:
    Problems with Meat by John A Scharffenberg, M.D.
    Nutrition for vegetarians by Agatha Thrash, M.D.

CHEESE

A summary of the objectionable features of hard or
ripened cheeses includes the following:

1. The putrefactive process results in the production
   of amines, ammonia, irritating fatty acids
   (butyric, caproic, caprylic, etc.) The carbohydrate is converted to lactic acid. These are
   all waste products which cause irritation to nerves
   and gastro-intestinal tract.
2. Migraine headaches can be caused by tyramine, one of
   the toxic amines produced in cheese.
3. Certain of the amines can interact with the nitrates
   present in the stomach to form nitrosamine, a cancer
   producing agent.
4. An intolerance to lactose, the chief carbohydrate of
   cheese and milk, is probably the most common food
   sensitivity in America.
5. Rennet is used in cheese making. It comes from the
   stomach of calves, lambs, or pigs.

REORDER FORM

OF THESE YE MAY FREELY EAT JoAnn Rachor   2.95

HOME REMEDIES   Drs. Agatha and Calvin Thrash   8.95

NUTRITION for VEGETARIANS   Drs. Agatha and
    Calvin Thrash   8.95

NATURAL REMEDIES   Drs. Agatha and Calvin Thrash   6.95

ANIMAL CONNECTION   Drs. Agatha and Calvin Thrash   4.95

EAT FOR STRENGTH COOKBOOK   Agatha Thrash, M.D.
    (reg. or oil free)   7.95

PROBLEMS WITH MEAT   John Scharffenberg M.D.   4.95

SUNLIGHT   Zane Kime, M.D., M.S.   11.95

HOW TO STOP SMOKING   1.50

CHILDERS DIET TO STOP ARTHRITIS   Norman
    Childers, Ph.D.   8.95

DROP YOUR BLOOD PRESSURE Lloyd Rosenvold, M.D.   2.75

DIET,CRIME AND DELINQUENCY   5.95

Family Health Publications
13062 Musgrove Highway
Sunfield, MI. 48890

Total _____

Postage _____

(.95 1st book,
.35 ea add. book)

Tax _____

(Mich.Res. 4%)

Enclosed _____

86

INDEX

HOW TO ORDER THIS BOOK

**Available at leading bookstores, health food stores,
or Adventist book centers.**

- or -

Send $2.95 (plus postage & handling—95¢ for first book, 35¢ for
each additional book) to:

Family Health Publications
13062 Musgrove Hwy.
Sunfield, MI 48890

- or -

MMI Press
Aldworth Road □ P.O. Box 279
Harrisville, NH 03450

WHOLESALE ORDERS: Use first address above.
Standard wholesale discount applies, plus actual postage and $1.50 handling.

DISTRIBUTORS: Please inquire at first address above,
or phone (205) 623-3720.